The DUTIES *of* CHRISTIANS

ENFORCED & ENJOINED

GREAT CHRISTIAN BOOKS
LINDENHURST, NEW YORK

The DUTIES of CHRISTIANS

CHRISTIANS

ENFORCED & ENJOINED

A Careful Exegetical Study of 1 Peter 5:1-5

Foreword by William Shishko

JOHN BROWN

Great Christian Books
is an imprint of Rotolo Media
160 37th Street Lindenhurst, New York 11757
(631) 956-0998

Brown, John, 1784 – 1858
The Duties of Christians—Enforced and Enjoined / by John Brown
p. cm.
A "A Great Christian Book" book
GREAT CHRISTIAN BOOKS an imprint of Rotolo Media
ISBN 978-1-61010-012-0
Recommended Dewey Decimal Classifications: 202, 230
Suggested Subject Headings:
1. Christianity—The Bible—Doctrines
2. Religion—Christian—Christianity & Christian theology
I. Title

Book and cover design for this title are by Michael Rotolo, www.michaelrotolo.com. It is typeset in the Minion typeface by Adobe Inc. and is quality-manufactured in the United States on acid-free paper stock. To discuss the publication of your Christian manuscript or out-of-print book, please contact Great Christian Books.

Manufactured in the United States of America

CONTENTS

FOREWORD

Years ago when I read the John Brown (of Edinburgh)'s commentary on I Peter 5:1-5 as part of his two volume commentary on I Peter published by the Banner of Truth Trust, I relished its careful exegetical treatment of this key New Testament passage which deals with the character, work, and relationship of church officers to the people they serve, with the attitude that people ought to have toward their church officers, and with the duty of mutual submission each owes to the other. Since that time I have earnestly wished that this chapter could be published as a separate, stand-alone volume. Its worth for initiating pastors and elders, for officer training, for church membership preparation, and for classes on these all-important subjects is unmatched. There is simply nothing like it in any other comparably sized volume.

Now, through the fine service of Great Christian Books, that volume has been made available and is now in your hands.

John Brown (of Edinburgh) lived from 1784 to 1858. For the last twenty-nine years of his life he ministered in Edinburgh, Scotland, where he became known for a pulpit ministry that was rich in careful, systematic treatment of the biblical texts on which he preached, and also for warm, wise, practical application that grew out of those carefully interpreted texts. Brown was a Puritan of his day. His skills were recognized in 1834 when he was appointed as Scotland's first Professor of Exegetical Theology. He served in that capacity as an instructor at the Divinity Hall of the

Secession Church until his death less than a quarter century later. In that time he produced eleven volumes of expository works on the New Testament, three of which were on I Peter. Embedded in those volumes is the material on I Peter 5:1-5

Although carrying the imposing subtitle, *The Ecclesiastical Duties of Christians Enjoined and Enforced*, Brown deals clearly and comprehensively with the duties of elders, the duties of church members to office bearers, and "mutual duties." One can easily see the relevance of all of this material to church life today—and in any day.

Brown convincingly affirms and defends the plurality of elders for the healthy government of a local congregation. However, it is his development of the pastoral role of all elders that is so rich and compelling. In showing how the work of rule and the work of shepherding are, essentially, two sides of the same biblical coin Brown, offers a portrait of elder service that, if heeded, would transform the mindset and labors of local elderships. Indeed, this material is of inestimable value in helping to flesh out the rather stark descriptions of "The Ruling Elder" in standard books of Church Order for Presbyterian Churches. (Those of continental Reformed background will here receive much of the exegetical and theological material which undergirds the pastoral role of elders as developed in their historic Church Order.)

In considering the work of superintendence (or oversight, i.e. the "episcopal" function of all elders), Brown gives a lucid development of the meaning of reception of church members on the basis of credible professions of faith. He steers the biblical course between "regenerate church membership" and "easy

believe-ism". Then, in the correlative section on the authority
church leaders have over their members, he demonstrates with
equal lucidity that church authority is not "magisterial and legislative", but "ministerial and declarative." One is hard pressed to
find this teaching (that is absolutely critical to the right exercise
of church authority) presented more simply and convincingly
anywhere else.

Brown presents thoughtful and heart-probing sections on
the character which elders are to bear, i.e. serving "not under
compulsion, but willingly…; not for shameful gain, but eagerly;
not domineering over those in your charge, but being examples to
the flock." (ESV). Here is good preventive medicine to help guard
against the painfully common abuse of church power that is the
stuff of authoritarianism and coltishness. Brown's exegetical work
is solid. His applications and the way he expresses them come
from a man with both pastoral experience and a pastor's heart.

Brown defends the view (convincingly, in my opinion) that
"likewise, you younger, submit yourselves to (the) elder" is, in fact
speaking of the submission of church members to their ordained
elders (a view represented in, among other Bible versions, the
ESV). He helpfully distinguishes between submission to elders as
individuals and as an eldership. And most important, he shows
how this submission, when it is rendered to rightly exercised rule
is, in fact, submission to Christ. How much we need to hear and
apply this in contemporary church life.

And in the final section on the duties owed by all to all
within the Church, Brown offers what is, in essence, an application of Ephesians 4:1-3. His development of the meaning of

humility is, arguably, the very heart of this entire exposition. It gives material for many sermons, and for even more broken-hearted trips to the cross of the self-denying Christ. Culminating in "Oh, happy the church, where all the elders and all the members are habitually under the influence of Christian humility!", this precious exposition calls us all to seek such grace and to pray and to labor for such churches.

Pastors— Break into your busy schedules to read this book, to be instructed by it, to be challenged by it, and to be reminded by it of the beauty of biblically ordered church life. You will be encouraged!

Elderships— Work through this material prayerfully, humbly, and with the goal of being reformed by it. Your church government will be revived!

Church members— Savor this biblical and theological feast over against the junk food of so many loose contemporary treatments of the Christian church and its organizational life. You will be nourished! Use this for preparing church members, for Sunday School classes, in portions for bulletin inserts, and in any way that will get its precious contents out. I am convinced that the widespread use of this classic treatment by Brown will serve the reformation and reviving of the Christian Church in ways we so desperately need—and for which we should fervently pray.

—William Shishko
Pastor of Orthodox Presbyterian Church
Franklin Square, New York

INTRODUCTION

THE ECCLESIASTICAL DUTIES OF CHRISTIANS
— ENJOINED and ENFORCED —

"The elders which are among you I exhort, who am also an elder, and a witness of the sufferings of Christ, and also a partaker of the glory that shall be revealed: feed the flock of God which is among you, taking the oversight thereof, not by constraint, but willingly; not for filthy lucre, but of a ready mind; neither as being lords over God's heritage, but being examples to the flock: and when the chief Shepherd shall appear, ye shall receive a crown of glory that fadeth not away. Likewise, ye younger, submit yourselves unto the elder. Yea, all of you be subject one to another, and be clothed with humility: for God resisteth the proud, and giveth grace to the humble."—1 Peter 1:1-5

In the preceding portions of this epistle, the Apostle has instructed those to whom he wrote in many of their religious and moral duties as individuals, and also in many of their duties as members of domestic and civil society. In the paragraph which comes now before us, he writes to them that they "may know how they ought to behave themselves in the house of God." He gives them a directory for their conduct, as office-bearers or private members of a Christian church. The duties of office-bearers in the church to those committed to their charge, and the duties of the members of the church, both to their office-bearers and to each other, are here very succinctly stated, and very powerfully enforced.

With regard to the office-bearers of the church, here termed "the elders," the whole of their duty is represented as consisting in acting the part of shepherds and overseers of that portion of the flock or family of God committed to their care; the temper or disposition in which this duty must be discharged is described, both negatively and positively, "not by constraint, nor for filthy lucre, not as lords of God's heritage," but "willingly, of a ready mind, as examples of the flock;" and to secure a conscientious performance of this duty, besides employing his personal influence with them, as being himself "also an elder, and a witness of the sufferings of Christ, and a partaker of the glory which shall be revealed," the Apostle turns their attention to the peculiar character of the church as "the flock," and "heritage of God," and to the rich reward which shall be conferred on the faithful under-shepherds and overseers, by the chief Shepherd and Overseer at his "glorious appearing," and their "gathering together to him."

With regard to the members of the church, who, with a reference, we apprehend, to their office-bearers being termed "elders," [1] are described by the correlative appellation "younger," [2] or juniors, just as if the office-bearers had been termed fathers, they would have been termed children; their duty to their office-bearers is described under the general word, "submission."

The duty of all connected with the Christian church, whether as officers or private members, is enjoined under the expression, mutual subjection. Humility is enjoined as necessary in order to the right discharge of all these classes of duties; and the cultivation of this disposition, so requisite to the prosperity and good order of the church, is recommended by a strong statement, couched in the language of Old Testament scripture, of the peculiar complacency with which God regards the humble, and the contemptuous reprobation with which he regards the proud. Such is a brief analysis of the paragraph, which we shall find of use in guiding our thoughts in our subsequent illustrations. The peculiar duties of the rulers in the Christian church, the peculiar duties of the members of the Christian church, and the duties common to both,—these are the important topics to which in the sequel your attention will be successively directed.

PART ONE

OF THE DUTIES OF THE RULERS IN THE CHRISTIAN CHURCH

And first, of the duties of the rulers in the Christian church. For the right illustration of this part of our subject, it will be requisite that we consider, first, the appellation here given to those who rule in the Christian Church, and to whom that appellation properly belongs; secondly, the duty which they are required to perform; thirdly, the manner in which that duty ought to be performed; and lastly, the motives by which the performance of this duty in this manner is enforced.

CHAPTER ONE

THE APPELLATION HERE GIVEN TO THE RULERS IN THE CHRISTIAN CHURCH,—"ELDERS"

1. THE ORIGIN AND MEANING OF THE APPELLATION

The appellation here given to the rulers in the church, those who were to act the part of shepherds to it, as the flock of God, the part of overseers to it as the family of God, is that of "elders," or presbyters, which last term is just the Greek word with an English termination. "The elders, or presbyters, who are among you, I exhort." The word in its literal signification describes the persons to whom it is given as of comparatively advanced age. As rule ought to be committed only to those who are characterized by knowledge and wisdom; as, in ordinary circumstances, these are not to be expected in a high degree in very young persons, since both qualifications are generally understood to be of somewhat difficult acquirement and slow growth; as in the simplest form of human governments, the domestic, the elder members of the society are the ruling members in it; and as, where the ruling orders in civil society are elective, they are generally chosen from among those of at least mature age, it is not at all wonderful that the appellation, primarily significant merely of superior age, should have been very generally employed to denote superior dignity and authority. The Hebrew ordinary civil rulers are termed "the elders of Israel." The assembled magistrates of Rome were termed the senate or meeting of elders, and its individual members senators. In some of the most extensively spoken continental languages, the title expressive of dignity and rule, and which we would render by the word lord, actually signifies just elder; [3] and the English term "alderman," descriptive of municipal authority and power in many cities, is just an antiquated form of the words "elder man."

It has been the opinion of some of the most judicious and learned students of the history of apostolical and primitive Christianity, that the constitution of the Christian church was, under apostolic guidance, "modelled for the most part after that religious community with which it stood in the closest connection, the Jewish synagogue; such modifications, however, taking place as were required by the nature and design of the Christian community, and the new and peculiar spirit by which it was animated." [4] In this case it would have been strange if the designation of the managers of the affairs of the Jewish Synagogue, "elders," had not been transferred to the superintendents of the Christian church. And we cease to wonder that we have no particular account of the formal establishment of the office of elders, it being very probable, that the existing order of things in the synagogues for religious instruction and discipline, which had been originally organized by inspired men, was silently, and without the formality of express legislative enactment, transferred, under apostolic superintendence, and with apostolic sanction, to the meetings of the disciples, the churches of Christ.

With the exceptions of "the deacons," a term signifying ministers or servants, who obviously as deacons had no part in the government of the church, "the elders" appear to be the only ordinary set of office-bearers in the apostolic and primitive churches. In an inspired account of the constitution of the Christian church, we are informed, when her only Lord and King ascended on high, "he gave," that is, he appointed, and qualified, and commissioned, "some Apostles, and some prophets, and some evangelists, and some pastors and teachers, for the perfecting of the saints, for the work of the ministry, for the edification of the body of Christ." [5] The office of the Apostles was altogether peculiar, and they who filled it were intended for the benefit of the church in all ages. They were the accredited messengers of Christ. They had his mind.[6] He spake by them, and wrought by them; and though they had long left this world, in their inspired writings they are still in the church, according to the promise of their Lord, "sitting on thrones, judging the twelve tribes of spiritual

Israel;" and in the same writings they are still "going into all the world, proclaiming the gospel;" and their Lord by his Spirit is with them, and will continue to be with them till the end of the world. The prophets necessarily disappeared when the prophetic spirit was withdrawn. The evangelists seem not to have been properly office-bearers in the church, but messengers from the church to the world lying under the wicked one; and the missionary, in the later ages of the church, seems to fill a place similar to that occupied by the evangelist in the primitive age. The pastors and teachers, which terms do not seem to denote two distinct classes of men, but two functions of the same general class, appear to be the only permanent ordinary office-bearers appointed for the putting and keeping in fit order, for that is the meaning of the word rendered "perfecting the saints," those sanctified in Christ Jesus; called to be saints, the disciples, the brethren; for the work of the ministry, for the edifying of the body of Christ; and, as we shall see by and by, these pastors and teachers were just the same persons who are here called elders.

In another inspired account by the same Apostle of the constitution of the Christian church, we are informed that "God hath set some in the church,—first, Apostles; secondarily, prophets; thirdly, teachers; after that miracles: then gifts of healing, helps, governments, diversities of tongues." [7] Here it is plain that the Apostles, the prophets, the workers of miracles of various kinds, do not belong to the permanent order of the church. Fact has decided that question. "Helps," or helpers, seem plainly the deacons; while the teachers and the governments are just the same class of persons as the pastors and teachers, their two different functions of instruction and rule being mentioned in an inverse order in the two cases.

As this order of men received the appellation of elders on the same ground as rulers have generally been designated by some such title, [8] and as occupying in the church materially the same place as the Jewish elders did in the synagogue; so, from the great design of their appointment, they are not unfrequently termed bishops, which is an anglicised Greek word, disguised in this way in our version of the New Testament, there is reason to believe, to serve a purpose, and an unworthy one, but which means neither more nor less than our English word "overseers;" by which word indeed, to serve a purpose too, and the same one, it is in one or two cases rendered. That the only bishops known in the New Testament are the same class of persons who are termed elders, may be made very plain in a very few words. Paul, on his journey from Macedonia to Jerusalem, sent from Miletus, and called the elders of Ephesus: and, when these elders had come, he exhorted them to "take heed to all the flock over which the Holy Ghost had made them overseers, bishops." Paul, writing to Titus, states, that he had left him in Crete, to ordain elders in every city. He enumerates the qualifications of an elder, and then adds, "for a bishop," or overseer, "must be blameless," etc. [9] If this does not identify the bishop with the elder, what can do it? Suppose a law pointing out the qualifications of a sheriff were to say— A sheriff must be a man of good character, great activity, and resolute spirit, for it is highly necessary the chief magistrate of the county should be of unspotted reputation, would it be possible to come to any other conclusion than that, in the eye of the legislature, the sherriff and the first magistrate of the county were just two names for the same officer? How inconsistent would it be to say to a captain —In appointing sergeants you must appoint only men of such qualifications, specifying them, and then add, for these are the proper qualifications for a general or a field-marshal? But we need not go farther than the text in search of the identification of the Christian elder, and the apostolic bishop, and the apostolic pastor. "The elders I exhort: Act the part of pastors to the flock; shepherd them, acting the part of bishops, or overseers."[10] The elders, in other words, are exhorted to act the part of good pastors, good bishops.

The whole care of a Christian church as a spiritual society, including instruction, superintendence, and discipline, was committed to these elders, though it is very probable that in the primitive churches, as among us, there were authorized public teachers who were not elders, and had no share in the management of any church.

It is plain there was a plurality of such elders in every church. These formed the eldership or presbytery of that church. In the church of Jerusalem, when met for government, we find just the Apostles, extraordinary officers, the elders, ordinary officers, and the brethren or church members who listened to their deliberations, and to whom their decision seemed good. We know there were deacons in that church; but their office was not rule, and therefore they are not named. The church of Philippi, which was set in order by the Apostle, was composed of "the saints in Christ Jesus," the private members; "the bishops," overseers; elders, who ruled; and "the deacons," who served. [11]

While the entire spiritual charge of the church was committed to the presbytery or meeting of elders, what we are in the habit of calling the session, there is evidence, not that the elders were divided into a pastor or pastors who only taught, and bishops who ruled; but that, while all the elders severally and in a body superintended and ruled, there were some of these elders "who labored in word, and doctrine," devoting themselves chiefly to the exposition and enforcement of the doctrine and law of our Lord Jesus.

It is comparatively a modern, at any rate it is not a New Testament usage, to apply the term "pastor" exclusively to those teaching elders, that term naturally expressing the whole work of the Christian eldership; and, like the kindred term "bishop," being given in the New Testament to Christian elders indiscriminately. But that such a distinction as that between elders who taught and ruled, and elders who only ruled, existed from the beginning, is made probable by the reasonableness and almost necessity of the arrangement, and its obvious tendency to secure the gaining in the best way and in the greatest degree the ends of the Christian eldership; and appears to me proved by the passage in the First Epistle to Timothy, v. 17, of which, after all that has been said for the purpose of reconciling it to the episcopal or independent order of church polity, I am disposed to say, with Dr. Owen, that "on the first proposal of this text, that 'the elders who rule well are worthy of double honors, especially those who labor in word and doctrine,' a rational man who is unprejudiced, who never heard of the controversy about ruling elders, can hardly avoid an apprehension that there are two sorts of elders; some of whom labor in word and doctrine, and some who do not so."

2. QUALIFICATIONS OF CHRISTIAN ELDERS

With regard to the qualifications which are necessary for filling the office of a Christian elder, we have full information in the epistles of Paul to Timothy and Titus. "This is a true saying," says he, in his First Epistle to Timothy, iii. 1, "If a man desire the office of a bishop," an overseer, an elder, in the Christian church, "he desireth a good work. A bishop then must be blameless, the husband of one wife, vigilant, sober, of good behavior, given to hospitality, apt to teach; not given to wine, no striker, not greedy of filthy lucre; but patient, not a broiler, not covetous; one that ruleth well his own house, having his children in subjection with all gravity; for if a man know not how to rule his own family, how shall he take care of the house," the family, "of God? Not a novice," a late convert, "lest being lifted up with pride, he fall into the condemnation of the devil. Moreover, he must have a good report of those who are without; lest he fall into reproach and the snare of the devil." "Ordain elders," says he to Titus, "in every city, as I had appointed thee. If any be blameless, the husband of one wife, having faithful children, not accused of riot, or unruly. For a bishop must be blameless, as the steward of God; not self-willed, not soon angry, not given to wine, no striker, not given to filthy lucre; but a lover of hospitality, a lover of good men, just, holy, temperate; holding fast the faithful word as he hath been taught, that he may be able by sound doctrine both to exhort and to convince gainsayers." These are qualifications which are requisite in all elders, though some of them may be required in a higher degree in those who are called to labor in word and doctrine.

3. OF THE MANNER IN WHICH ELDERS WERE INVESTED WITH OFFICE

With regard to the manner in which the elders were invested with these offices in the apostolic church, we have comparatively little information. We know that Paul and Barnabas ordained elders every church which was gathered by their ministry; and that Titus was enjoined by Paul to ordain elders in every city where the gospel had taken root. But we should undoubtedly err, were we concluding that these offices were appointed by the Apostles or evangelists, whatever their authority might be, without consulting the brethren. When we reflect on the nature and design of a Christian church, and take into consideration the probable method of electing an Apostle in room of Judas, and the distinctly recorded facts respecting the election of the deacons, we cannot doubt that the elders were elected by the brethren from among themselves, and presented by them to the Apostles, evangelists, or other church rulers, who, with fasting, prayer, and laying on of hands, solemnly set them apart to the discharge of the functions of the office to which they had been chosen; thus, in the most impressive way, intimating their conviction of their fitness for the office, and their cordial acknowledgment of them as fellowlaborers, and commending them to the special care and blessing of their common Lord. So much for the elders to whom the Apostle here addresses so solemn and affectionate an exhortation.

CHAPTER TWO

OF THE DUTIES OF CHRISTIAN ELDERS

1. OF THE FIGURATIVE TERMS IN WHICH THESE DUTIES ARE DESCRIBED, ACTING THE PART OF A SHEPHERD AND AN OVERSEER

Let us now, in the second place, attend to the duty which is here enjoined on these elders. They are enjoined to "feed the flock of God, and to take the oversight of it." The two words employed to describe the elder's duty, are suited to the two figurative representations here given us of the objects of their care. If viewed as the flock of God, they are to feed, or rather, as the word properly signifies, they are to act the part of shepherds to them. If viewed as the property of God, or the family of God, they are to act the part of overseers in reference to them. The Israelitish people are often in Scripture termed the flock of God, and their rulers appointed by him, their shepherds; they are represented also as the peculiar property and as the family of God, and their rulers as overseers, tutors, governors, appointed by the Father. The Christian church is the anti-type of the Israelitish people. The whole body of believers are the flock of God, the property of God, the family of God; for in the new economy all things are of God by Christ Jesus. We are Christ's, Christ is God's. Jesus Christ who laid down his life for the sheep, is the Great Shepherd, the Chief Shepherd, whose own the sheep are. To him is committed the care of the property which was purchased, redeemed to God, by his blood; and he, as the Son, is entrusted with the management of the whole family called by his name. He is the shepherd, and bishop or overseer, of their souls.[12] Christian elders are here represented as under-shepherds, subordinate overseers; and their duty to that portion of the flock of God committed to their care, is what the Apostle here refers to.

It has, I believe, been very generally supposed by inter-preters, that the expression rendered "feed" refers solely to instruction; and that rendered by "taking oversight" to discipline and government. If the term "feed" adequately represented the force of the original term, there might be a good deal said for this mode of interpretation; for, no doubt, knowledge is mental food, and instruction is spiritual feeding; but the truth is, the word signifies, generally, act the part, discharge the duty, of a shepherd, and is ordinarily, when used in a figurative sense, significant of ruling, being applied to kings. To procure and administer food to the flock is an important part of the shepherd's duty, but it is not his only duty; he must strengthen the diseased and heal the sick, and bind up the broken, aud bring again that which was driven away, and seek that which was lost. He must go before them, and guide them, and govern them. The whole duties of the Christian eldership are included in shepherding the flock; and equally extensive is the other figurative representation of the elder superintending, that is, taking care of. If it refer to property, how can such a property, consisting of immortal minds, be taken care of? Must not instruction, putting them in the way of taking care of themselves, be a part of the overseer's work? and, if it refer to a family, must not the good steward, tutor, and overseer, the ruler over his master's family, not merely superintend the conduct of the household, keep them at their proper work, out of mischief, away from danger, but "give to every one his portion of meat in due season?"[13] The first term does not, then, exclusively refer to instruction; nor the second to superintendence and government. They are two figurative representations, each of them embracing the whole compass of the duty of the eldership of a Christian church.

2. OF THE DUTIES THEMSELVES

The whole of the duties of the Christian eldership do, however, naturally enough range themselves under the two heads of instruction and discipline, or superintendence and government, and to these in their order I wish very briefly to call your attention.

1. INSTRUCTION

First, then, Christian elders are to act the part of shepherds and overseers to those under their care, by providing and administering instruction to them. It is an important part of the shepherd's duty to find wholesome nourishing pasture for his flock. It is an important part of the duty of the overseer of the family to see, that every member of it be furnished with a sufficient portion of suitable food. "The truth as it is in Jesus," the doctrine and the law of Christ, serve in the spiritual economy a purpose analogous to that which food does in the animal economy. Suitable wholesome food must be eaten and digested, in order to health and bodily growth, and, indeed, to the continuance of animal life; and Divine truth must be understood and believed, and thus become influential on the intellect, and conscience, and affections, in order to the continuance of spiritual life, and to the healthy exercise of the functions of the new creature. The private members of the church, as well as the ministers of Jesus Christ, are "nourished up by the words of faith and good doctrine," whereunto they attain; and the "new-born babes grow" by "the sincere milk of the word," which the instincts of their new nature lead them to desire.

Regularly and effectually to meet this exigence is one leading object of the Christian eldership; and where suitable provision is not made for securing the growing intelligence of the members of a Christian church, there must be, on the part of the eldership, most blamable neglect of duty.

When the disciples come together on the first day of the week to observe the ordinances, the ordinance of "doctrine" or teaching must be attended to; and the assembled brethren must be taught to hold fast and observe all things, whether doctrine, law, or institution, which the Lord has commanded them. On these occasions, the elders who labor in word and doctrine should be prepared, after close study and fervent prayer, to present to their brethren a clear and impressive exhibition of the meaning, evidence, and practical bearing of some of our Lord's doctrines, or a perspicuous and practical explanation and enforcement of some of our Lord's laws, having a reference to what they know to be the necessities and capacities of their audience, taking care not to confine themselves to a few topics to descant on which may be peculiarly easy to themselves, and palatable to their hearers, but endeavoring, as much as possible, to bring out in the course of these exercises, so far as they have discovered it, "the whole counsel of God;" and withholding nothing that can be profitable, whether it may be pleasing or otherwise. When we consider how much the great body of Christians, belonging to the classes whose time is chiefly devoted to obtaining the necessaries and comforts of life for themselves and families, must be dependent on the instructions received on the Lord's-day for their knowledge of Christian truth, the importance of Christian teachers endeavoring, on such occasions, to communicate the largest possible amount of distinct impressive instruction, both doctrinal and practical, must appear great indeed.

The Christian preacher, if he is really wise when teaching the people knowledge, will give good heed to his doctrine that it be wholesome and nourishing; and, if possible, palatable. He will seek to find out, first, true and important thoughts, and then plain acceptable words; and he will endeavor that his words be as goads, entering readily, and as riveted nails when they have entered, sticking fast. The teaching elder ill discharges this, his highest duty, who satisfies himself with common-place statement or empty declamation; or who spends the hours devoted to Christian instruction in metaphysical discussions, and "questions that profit not." It has been well said, "To preach, to show the extent of our learning or the subtlety of our wit, to blazon them in the eyes of the people with the beggarly accounts of a few words which glitter, but convey little light and less warmth, is a dishonest use of sacred time; it is not to preach the gospel, but ourselves:" it is not to feed, but to starve our hearers.

It is the duty of the Christian-teaching elder, not only thus to teach publicly on the Lord's-day, but also, as God gives opportunity, to teach from house to house, taking such opportunities for presenting Christian truth in a form more familiar than befits the character of public instruction, and more suited to the circumstances of the individuals addressed. It seems to me, also, that a Christian eldership are but following out the spirit of the injunction in the text, when they endeavor to secure, and earnestly recommend for the perusal of those under their care, the use of a collection of really good and appropriate books, fitted to promote the knowledge of Christian truth, the cultivation of Christian feeling, and the performance of Christian duty, by enabling their hearers better to understand the Bible.

The use of all appropriate means, especially the preaching of the word, for securing that the brethren under their care grow in accuracy and extent of Christian knowledge, must ever be considered, by the Christian eldership, as the fundamental part of their duty. The church is the school of Christ, and the elders are the schoolmasters. The maxim, that ignorance is the mother of devotion, is utterly inapplicable to the religion of Christ. Knowledge is necessary in order to faith; and a well instructed Christian mind is the only soil in which can grow and flourish the fair flowers and the rich fruits of devout feeling and holy conduct, "which are by Christ Jesus to the praise and glory of God."

The duty of instructing the brethren, lies with peculiar weight on the teaching elder. It is his business, his appropriate work, to which above all things he must give himself, and to which he must endeavor to make all things subservient. Whatever may be cursorily done, this must be done carefully; and he must "study to prove himself a workman that needs not to be ashamed, rightly dividing the word of truth." At the same time, every Christian elder, though not called to labor in word and doctrine, ought to endeavor to promote the instruction of the brethren. Every elder, or bishop, should be "apt to teach;" both able and disposed to communicate Christian instruction to his brethren. Indeed, till "the earth be full of the knowledge of the Lord as the waters cover the sea," it is the duty of every Christian man "to teach his neighbor, and every man his brother, saying, Know the Lord." And the Christian elder, whose ordinary and principal business is to superintend and govern, is not only warranted, but bound, to turn to account his interchange with the brethren in discharging his appropriate functions, for directly as well as indirectly endeavoring to promote their progress in that knowledge of God and our Lord Jesus Christ, through which, and through which alone, grace, mercy, and peace, can be multiplied to them; through which, and through which alone, they can become the holy, happy, active, useful persons, that all members of a Christian church ought to be.

This duty of instruction must be performed to *all* the flock. The command of the chief Shepherd is not only, "Feed my sheep," but "feed my lambs;"[14] and there does seem something wanting in a Christian church, where provision is not made, and made by the elders, directly or indirectly, personally or by guiding and superintending the exertions of others, for the instruction of the younger branches of the family. The instruction of Christian children is the appropriate work of Christian parents, and is never likely to be so efficiently performed as by them; but it seems plain, that not only is it the duty of Christian elders, in their work of superintending and governing, to see that parents discharge their obligations in this respect, but also, by a system of religious training, common to all the children connected with the church, not to supersede, but to assist and supplement, parental instruction.

In these remarks, I have been preaching chiefly to two individuals: "my true yoke-fellow, who serves with me as a son in the gospel of Jesus Christ," and myself. The next department of the discourse will be directed to the brethren of the eldership, who rule, though they do not labor in word and doctrine. But if those illustrations of the law of Christ in reference to elders, serve, as I hope they will, their proper purpose in us and in them, the congregation are likely to be fully as much the better for them, as for any sermons they have ever heard addressed more directly to themselves. The importance and the difficulty of rightly instructing a Christian congregation, especially such a congregation as this, consisting of so many individuals, placed in such a variety of circumstances, and possessed of such a variety of capacities and tastes for religious mental training, are, I trust, justly estimated by your ministers; and it is our earnest wish, "by the manifestation of the truth, to commend ourselves to every man's conscience in the sight of God." We would not willingly conceal nor corrupt any portion of the doctrines or the laws of our Lord. We wish to preach Christ, the sole authoritative teacher and lawgiver, the sole atoning Savior, the sole sovereign Lord; "warning every man, and teaching every man in all wisdom, that we may present every man perfect in Christ Jesus." "Being allowed of God to be put in trust with the gospel, we would so speak, not as pleasing men, but God, who trieth the hearts." Sensible of the importance of rightly dividing the word of truth, we would "give attendance to meditation and to reading," as well as to exhortation and doctrine; we would "shun profane and vain babblings, and speak the things, and only the things, that become sound doctrine;" in our teaching, "showing incorruptness, and sound speech that cannot be condemned."[15]

Help us, brethren, with your prayers. Pray for us, that our understandings may be more and more opened, that we may understand the Scriptures; that, being more thoroughly and extensively taught of God ourselves, we may be the better fitted for teaching you. "Brethren, I beseech you, for the Lord Jesus' sake, and for the love of the Spirit, that ye strive together with us in your prayers for us that our minds and hearts may be more and more filled with the truth, and the love of it; and that utterance may be given us, that we may open our mouths boldly, to make known the mystery of the gospel; that the word of the Lord may have free course and be glorified among us;"[16] that we may speak it as it ought to be spoken, with firm faith and melting affection. It is your interest as well as ours, that you should be thus employed. "Were people much in the duty of prayer for their teachers, not only would the ministers be the better for it, the people themselves would receive back their prayers with much gain into their bosom. They would have the returned benefit of it, as the vapors that go from below fall down again upon the earth in sweet showers, and make it fruitful. If there went up many prayers for ministers, their doctrine would drop as the rain, and distill as the dew, and the sweet influence of it would make fruitful the valleys, the humble hearts receiving it."[17] And we pledge ourselves to reciprocate your friendly supplications. "God forbid that we should sin against the Lord by ceasing to pray for you." Daily will we "bow our knees unto the Father of our Lord Jesus Christ, of whom the whole family in heaven and in earth are named," that the gospel may come to you not in word only, but in power, with the

Holy Ghost, and much assurance: "that the God of our Lord Jesus Christ, the Father of glory, may give to you the spirit of wisdom and revelation in the knowledge of him; that the eyes of your understanding being enlightened, ye may know what is the hope of his calling, and what the riches of his inheritance in the saints, and what is the exceeding greatness of his power in them that believe," transforming them by the renewing of their mind, purifying their hearts by faith, filling them with all joy and peace in believing; and "that he would grant you, according to the riches of his glory, to be strengthened with might by his Spirit in the inner man; that Christ may dwell in your hearts by faith; that ye, being rooted and grounded in love, may be able to comprehend with all saints what is the breadth, and length, and depth, and height; and to know the love of Christ, which passeth knowledge, being filled with all the fullness of God." [18]

2. SUPERINTENDENCE

I proceed to remark, in the second place, that Christian elders are to act the part of shepherds and overseers to those under their care, by superintending and governing them. The shepherd has but imperfectly done his work when he has procured for, and administered to, his flock, wholesome nourishment. He must watch over them; he must not allow either wolves or goats to mix with them, and, should such find their way among them, he must use appropriate means to get rid of them; he must endeavor to prevent the sheep from straying, and, when they do wander, he must employ every proper method to bring them back; he must endeavor to preserve them from the attacks of disease, and administer suitable preventives and medicines for prevailing maladies; and even at personal hazard he must protect them from those beasts of prey who go about seeking to devour them. The overseer or steward has but imperfectly done his duty, when he has secured that the children are furnished with suitable instruction. It is his business to see that they pay a proper attention to the instruction prepared for them, and make due improvement. He must look to the formation of their character and the direction of their conduct. He must take care that they are neither idle nor mischievous; that they are kind to each other, and dutiful to all. Both the shepherd and the overseer must be superintendents and governors. In like manner, the furnishing the flock and family of God with an abundance of wholesome spiritual nourishment, though, as we have seen, one most important part of the duty of Christian elders, is by no means the whole of it. The elders are not only to "speak the word of God" to their charge; they are to "have," hold, or exercise, "rule over them;" they are to "care" for them, to "watch for their souls."[19]

The duties of rule or superintendence which devolve on Christian elders, may be considered in reference either to the Christian society over which they are placed viewed as a body, or to the individual members of that body. The fundamental part of this duty, so far as the society is concerned, and without a careful performance of which the other duties, whether to the society or to its members, can only be very unsatisfactorily discharged, is to take care that it be composed of the right materials. How could a shepherd manage a flock, composed of swine as well as of sheep? or how could an overseer manage a family, into which aliens, "strange children," were continually intruding themselves? Nothing can be plainer from the New Testament than this, that though Christian churches are the grand means for converting the world, the apparent conversion of the worldling must precede, not follow, his admission into the church. The great ends to be gained by Christian churches, whether in reference to their Lord, as living manifestations of his truth, and holiness, and grace; or in reference to their members—their edification in knowledge, faith, love, and Christian excellence and usefulness generally; or in reference to the world lying under the wicked one —their conviction and conversion,—will be secured just in the degree in which these societies are formed of men who really know and churches of Christ must be churches, that is, assemblies, societies, of saints, "separated persons," "devoted persons," "sanctified persons," separated from the present evil world; devoted to the service of God and his Son; sanctified by the influence of the Holy Ghost. Such are the designations given the members of the church in the apostolic epistles. "Beloved of God, called to be saints, sanctified in Christ Jesus, calling on his name, brethren, faithful, elect," that is, selected "by a spiritual separation to the obedience of faith, and sprinkling of the blood of Jesus Christ, men that have obtained like precious faith with the Apostles."

The office-bearers are "stewards of the mysteries of Christ." It is their business "to take the precious from the vile." They are builders of the temple of the Lord, which ought to be composed of "living stones," of precious materials; and they must take care that the materials they employ in building it up be not "wood, hay, and stubble," but "gold, silver, and precious stones." [20] Christian elders should admit none to the communion of the church except those who make an intelligent and credible profession of the faith; who, in the judgment of an enlightened charity, are Christians in the only true sense of that word; and should, as in every church will be the case, persons be admitted who are not what they appear to be, when the real character is developed, the elders ought, in the exercise of an impartial discipline, to exclude them from a place they should never have occupied; and by continuing to occupy which, while their characters remain unchanged, they can only do injury to all the interests which the Christian church is meant to subserve.

Christian elders are to seek to promote this healthy state of a Christian church, not only by careful admission and discipline, but by such a clear and faithful exhibition of the holy doctrines and laws of Christ, and by keeping the society so actively engaged in the great object of their association, the promoting each other's edification, and the advancing the cause of Christ in the world, as will make ungodly men little desirous, while they continue ungodly, to enter such a society; and if, by a mistake on either side, they have entered it, will make them soon feel that they can be comfortable in it in no other way than by imbibing the spirit and submitting to the law of its great Founder.

It is the duty of Christian elders not only thus to endeavor that the society be composed only of right members, but in all their meetings to preside among them, keeping before them the law of Christ, taking care that they "continue steadfastly" in the observance of Christian institutions, keeping the ordinances committed to them by the Apostles, holding the traditions as taught in the Scriptures, the "Apostles' doctrine, the fellowship, the breaking of bread, and the prayers;" that they do all things as a body which Christ Jesus has commanded them, and that they do them all "decently, and in order."

But the Christian elders must not only thus shepherd the flock of Christ, oversee the family of God, viewed as an organized body, but they must act the part of shepherds and overseers to the individuals of which that flock and family are composed. This is indeed necessarily implied in the right discharge of their duty to the society as a society; for how can a society be kept pure but by its members being such as they should be; and how can this be secured but by superintending and watching individual conduct? The spiritual shepherd must "look well to his flock, and know the state of his herd." How otherwise can he "strengthen the diseased, heal the sick, bind up that which is broken, and bring again that which is driven away;" how is he to "warn the unruly, to comfort the feeble-minded, and to support the weak? [21] It is the duty of the Christian elder not impertinently to iutrude into private affairs, but carefully and affectionately to watch the whole conduct of those under his care, and to administer caution, encouragement, advice, comfort, rebuke, and exhortation, as circumstances require; and to do all this as an undershepherd, an appointed overseer, in the name of Him, who, counting him trustworthy, has put him into this ministry.

In thus taking care of the house of God by ruling it, Christian elders are never to forget the true nature of their rule: they are "men under authority." They are not arbitrary despots, they are not even constitutional law-givers; they are but constituted administrators of the law of the one Master, who is in heaven. The flock is to be managed according to the revealed will of the great, good, Proprietor-Shepherd, whose own the sheep are. The family is to be governed according to the distinctly declared mind of the one Father, who is in heaven.

But Christian elders, as well as those under their care, are to remember that they are *rulers* under him, that they must take their orders from him, that they are accountable to him, that the sheep are not to dictate to the shepherds, nor the children to the tutors and governors. If Christian elders seek to please even the members of the church in any other way than by pleasing them for their good, for edification, by declaring and executing the law of Christ, they will prove that they are not the servants of Christ, but the servants of men. The authority of Christian elders, though subordinate and deputed, is real authority; so that, in the right discharge of their official duties, "he that despiseth them despiseth not man but God." He that contemns the humblest subordinate magistrate, regularly appointed and acting within the limits of his delegated authority, is guilty of disobedience to the supreme power. Such is a short view of the duty of Christian elders, as shepherds of the flock, overseers of the family of

God, duty included under the two heads, instruction, and superintendence or government.

CHAPTER THREE

OF THE MANNER IN WHICH THESE DUTIES ARE TO BE PERFORMED

Let us now, in the third place, turn our attention to the account which the Apostle gives of the manner in which these duties should be performed. In discharging their duties, Christian elders are not to act "by constraint, but willingly; not for filthy lucre, but of a ready mind; neither as being lords over God's heritage, but being examples of the flock." 1 We shall consider shortly, in their order, these characteristics of the right mode of performing the duties of the Christian eldership.

1. "NOT BY CONSTRAINT, BUT WILLINGLY"

Christian elders are to shepherd the flock, and superintend the family of God, "not by constraint, but willingly." Some have supposed that these words refer rather to the flock or family than to the shepherds or overseers; that they describe rather the means to be employed than the temper to be cherished by Christian elders; that they intimate that the flock of Christ are to be ruled, not by *force*, but by *persuasion*; that they are to be drawn, not driven; and that the Christian shepherds are to take as beacons, not examples, those Jewish shepherds who "with force and with cruelty ruled" [22] the sheep of the Lord. This is unquestionably truth; important truth; but it cannot be brought out of the Apostle's words without using violence. The three double clauses, all of them, obviously refer to the state of the mind of the Christian elder in the discharge of his duty. Even some of those interpreters who have seen this clearly, have yet fallen into a slight misapprehension as to the precise meaning and reference of the words before us. From not noticing that these words are equally connected with both the figurative injunctions of the duties of the Christian elder, and from being more occupied with the sound than the sense of the phrase, "taking the oversight," it has been common to consider these words as describing exclusively the temper in which the office of the eldership should be undertaken, not the disposition in which its duties should be habitually performed. It is obvious, however, that it refers to "feed the flock of Christ," as well as to "taking the oversight;" and it is equally obvious, that the word rendered "taking the oversight" does not refer to a person's entering on the eldership, though very applicable to such a person, but to persons who are elders; and might have been still more literally rendered, "superintending them;" [23] that is, not so much undertaking, as exercising, superintendence.

The passage has often been quoted to prove, that no man should be compelled by ecclesiastical authority to take office in the church generally, or to take office in a particular church; but its bearing on this subject, though important, is indirect. The meaning is, that a Christian elder should perform his duties, not reluctantly, as something that he is obliged to do, but cheerfully, as something thal^ie delights to do; not as a task to a hard master that he must perform, but as an honorable and delightful service, which carries its reward in the satisfaction it affords. The more the Christian elder is constrained by a regard to the authority of Christ, a sense of his grace, and the love of the brotherhood, to the discharge of these duties, so much the better; but these are species of constraint that not only do not interfere with, but necessarily imply, willinghood. It is true of duty generally, and eminently true of the duties of the Christian eldership, that they have no value in the estimation of God, and are little likely to be effectual for answering their object, unless they proceed from a willing mind; unless, as the Apostle expresses it in the epistle to Philemon, they are, "not as it were of necessity, but willingly." The duties of the eldership must be performed not "grudgingly or of necessity; for God loveth a cheerful" doer, as well as a cheerful "giver." [24] A Christian elder, if he is what he should be, will be very thankful that God has given him a place in his house at all; and though sensible of the difficulties of his duties, and his unfitness for their right discharge, he will be still more grateful that he has been honored with office there. He will be disposed to adopt the Apostle's words, "I thank Christ Jesus our Lord, who has enabled me, for that he counted me trustworthy, faithful, putting me into the ministry." And with the psalmist, "What shall I render to the Lord for this benefit?" The spirit of the under shepherd should be that of the chief Shepherd, who, when called according to his covenant engagement to lay down his life for the sheep, was "not rebellious, neither turned away back," but said "Lo, I come;" "I have a baptism to be baptised with; and how am I straightened till it be accomplished!" [25] "There may be," as Archbishop Leighton says, "in a Christian elder, very great reluctance in engaging and adhering to the work, from a sense of the excellence of it, and his unfitness; and the deep apprehension of those high interests, the glory of God and the salvation of souls; and yet he enters and continues in it with this willingness of mind, with most single and earnest desires of doing all he can for God and the flock of God; only grieved that there is in him so little suitableness of heart, so little holiness and acquaintance with God for enabling him to it; but might he find that, he were satisfied; and in attendance upon that, goes on and waits, and is doing according to his little skill and strength, and cannot leave it; is constrained indeed, but all the constraint is love to Jesus, and for the sake of the souls He hath bought; a constraint far different from the constraint here discharged; yea, indeed, that very willingness which is opposed to that other constraint."

2. "NOT FOR FILTHY LUCRE, BUT OF A READY MIND"

Christian elders are to shepherd the flock, and superintend the family of God, not "for filthy lucre, but of a ready mind;" as well as "not from constraint, but willingly." The former clause, as we have just seen, is equivalent to—not reluctantly, but cheerfully. This seems equivalent to, not in a self-interested, mercenary disposition, but in a disinterested spirit of gratitude to God and love to the brethren.

There is nothing wrong in a Christian elder, who devotes his time and talents to the promotion of the good of the church over which he is placed, receiving, from the church's justice and gratitude, their sense of his claims on them, and their obligations to him, temporal support. It is the command of the Apostle, "Let him who is taught, communicate to him that teacheth in all good things." It is the ordination of our Lord, "that they who preach the gospel should live on the gospel," just as "they who ministered at the altar lived by the altar." Who goeth a warfare anytime at his own charges? who planteth a vineyard, and eateth not of the fruit thereof? or who feedeth a flock, and eateth not of the milk of the flock? Say I these things as a man? or saith not the law the same also? For it is written in the law of Moses, Thou shalt not muzzle the mouth of the ox that treadeth out the corn. Doth God care for oxen? or saith he it altogether for our sakes? For our sakes, no doubt, this is written, that he who ploweth should plow in hope; and he that thrasheth in hope should be partaker of his hope. If we have sown unto you spiritual things, is it a great thing if we shall reap your carnal things?"[26] These passages seem to refer to the teaching elder, whose whole attention is to be directed to reading and meditation in private, and to "word and doctrine," both publicly and from house to house; but it is plain that the elders who rule, if they are in circumstances in which they cannot devote the time necessary to the service of the church, without injustice to themselves and families, are equally entitled to support. This is implied in the injunction, "let the elders who rule well be counted worthy of double honor," obviously not excluding the honor of voluntary support, "especially those who labor in word or in doctrine."

But while all this is true, it is not less true that the duties of Christian elders must be performed "not for filthy lucre." No man must convert the Christian eldership into a trade, in this way "making gain of godliness." Even with those elders who are entirely dependent on their labors, who have no source of income but the effect of the authority and grace of Christ on the minds, and consciences, and hearts of those to whom they minister, the principle must be, "freely we have received, freely we give." And wherever sacred duties are performed from a regard to worldly gain, in whatever form, whether in the form of fixed stipend, or occasional gifts, or increased respectability of character and worldly influence, leading to success in worldly business, there is fearful desecration. The Apostle obviously lays much stress on this point. In his first Epistle to Timothy, iii. 3, he says, a bishop must "not be greedy of filthy lucre, nor covetous;" and in his Epistle to

Titus i. 7, he repeats the declaration. Such repeated warnings were not more than the case required. There has been too much of this in every age of the church, and the evil is not unknown even in our own times; nor is it confined within the limits of richly endowed churches, where its existence, if not less criminal than elsewhere, is less wonderful. It is a most deplorable thing when a regard to secular interest is allowed to interfere either with the declaration of Christian doctrine, or the administration of Christian discipline; when professed Christian teachers "prepare war against him that putteth not into their mouths," and "teach things that they ought not for filthy lucre's sake, through covetousness, with feigned words, making merchandise of their people, having hearts exercised to covetous practices, serving not the Lord Jesus Christ, but their own belly;" * and when the rulers of the church, from secular considerations, prefer one before another, and do anything in the administration of discipline by partiality; when "the watchmen are greedy dogs that can never have enough, all looking to their own way, every one for his gain from his quarter;" and when Malachi's question is an appropriate one, "Who is there among you that would shut the doors for naught? neither do ye kindle the fire on my altar for naught?" Balaam's resolution should be formed and kept, not only as it was by him in the letter, but as it was not by him, in the spirit. "If Balak would give me his house full of silver and gold, I cannot go beyond the word of the Lord my God, to do less or more." Yet it is very delightful to perceive that so many of our ministers are men who, with the same talents, and education, and effort, might have secured for themselves far higher secular advantages than they possess, or ever can expect to possess, as Christian elders. And the disinterestedness of many of our Christian elders who rule, but do not labor in word and doctrine, in not only cheerfully giving their unpaid, and often ill-estimated labor to the churches, but, in addition, being patterns to the believers in liberally giving of their substance to promote the support and extension of the cause of Christ, makes it very evident that they shepherd the flock, that they superintend the family of God, "not for filthy lucre, but of a ready mind." The Christian elder, when he becomes old and gray-headed, should be able to say with Samuel, "Behold, here I am; witness against me before the Lord; whose ox have I taken? or whose ass have I taken? or whom have I defrauded?" or with Paul, "I have coveted no man's silver or gold; I seek not yours, but you." [27] Disinterestedness, in opposition to mercenariness, should characterize the labors of the Christian elder. Regard to the Divine glory, gratitude for the Divine grace, love to the Savior who died, and to those for whom he died, eager desire that his name may not be blasphemed, through the inconsistent conduct of those who are called by it, and that it may be glorified in the holiness and happiness of his blood-bought heritage, and in bringing down the people in subjection to him, making them willing in the day of his power; these are the principles which should preside in the mind and heart of the Christian elder, and make him alert and cheerful in all the duties, however burdensome, of his official calling; producing a forwardness of mind far superior to what the stimulus of covetousness can create. Yes, as the good Archbishop says, "It is love, much love, which gives much unwearied care, and much skill in this charge. How sweet is it to him that loves to bestow himself, 'to spend and be spent,' upon his service whom he loves! Jacob, in the same kind of service, endured all, and found it light by reason of love, the cold of the nights and the heat of the days seven years for his Rachel, and they seemed to him but a few days, because he loved her. Love is the great endowment of a shepherd of Christ's flock. He says not to Peter, art thou wise, or learned, or eloquent? but 'lovest thou me?—lovest thou me?—lovest thou me?' Art thou of a ready mind? 'Feed my sheep: feed my lambs.'"

3. NOT AS LORDS OF GOD'S HERITAGE, BUT BEING EXAMPLES TO THE FLOCK

Christian elders are to shepherd the flock, and oversee the children of God, "not as lords of God's heritage, but being examples to the flock. These duties are to be performed not in a proud overbearing spirit. They are duties of *rule*, and therefore there is a temptation to pride in performing them. But the elders are to remember that, though they are rulers in, they are not lords over, the family of God. The Son alone is lord over his own house. We proclaim not ourselves lords, says the Apostle Paul; "we preach Jesus *the* Lord," the only Lord, the One Master and Proprietor. There were rulers in Israel; but Jehovah alone, in the highest sense of the word, was Israel's king. The soil was his, and so were the people. Of the spiritual Israel, Jehovah-Jesus is the proprietor and lord. He is Lord of all: he is our Lord, and we are all brethren. For the good of the whole, some of the brethren are called by him to rule under him, to administer his laws; but this lays no foundation for claiming to be lords of their faith. "The bride is the bridegroom's;" the church is the Lord's. The church does not belong to the elders, but the elders to the church. "All things are *yours*, and ye are Christ's, and Christ is God's." Diotrephes, who loved the pre-eminence, is the beacon, not the model, for Christian elders.

The Christian elder, even when he must "come with a rod," as but too often is necessary, should come "in love, and in the spirit of meekness." How beautifully did Paul, though in authority, and success, and gifts, "not behind the very chiefest of the Apostles," exemplify his beloved brother Peter's precept? He did not conduct himself as a lord over God's heritage. He disowned all claim to personal lordship over their faith. He sought not glory, but, when he might have used authority as an Apostle of Christ, was gentle among the disciples, even as a nurse cherisheth her children. And the servant of the Lord in every age must not be overbearing and ambitious: "he must not strive, but be gentle to all men, apt to teach, patient; in meekness instructing those who oppose themselves." He must never forget the words of the Master, "Ye know that the princes of the Gentiles exercise dominion over them, and they that are great exercise authority upon them. But it shall not be so among you: but whosoever will be great among you, let him be your minister; and whosoever will be chief among you, let him be your servant; even as the Son of man came not to be ministered unto, but to minister, and to give his life a ransom for many." [28]

Instead of acting as if they were lords of God's heritage, Christian elders are to perform their duties "as examples to the flock." In the careful discharge of their duty to those under their care, they are to teach them by example to perform the duties which they owe them and their Lord. By being dutiful to their people, they are to teach them to be dutiful to them. By being dutiful to Christ, they are to teach them to be obedient to him. And it deserves notice, that all the duties Christian elders are called on officially to discharge, are duties which the Christian brethren are substantially called on to perform. They are to "exhort one another daily while it is called today;" they are all of them to "look diligently, lest any man fail of the grace of God." And the graces, which are required in the Christian life, are just those which must be manifested in the right discharge of pastoral duty. [29]

A Christian elder cannot neglect duty, cannot commit sin of any kind, without doing more harm than a common church member; and no kind of neglect or fault is likely to exercise a more malignant influence, than those which refer to official obligations. The Christian elder, therefore, should seek to be "an example to the believers in word, in conversation, in charity, in spirit, in faith, in purity; showing himself a pattern of good works." What a blessed influence is the holy character and conduct of Christian elders calculated to diffuse through the church! In certain cases they should readily waive undoubted rights, that they may be the better able to give a needed example. They should imitate Paul: "Yourselves know," says he, to the Thessalonians, "how ye ought to follow us: for we behaved not ourselves disorderly among you; neither did we eat any man's bread for naught; but wrought with labor and travail night and day, that we might not be chargeable to any of you: not because we have not power, but to make ourselves an example unto you to follow us." [30] How happy is it when they can say, "We beseech you be followers of us as dear children; be followers of us even as we also are of Christ!" After a Christian elder has said to those under his care, "Whatsoever things are true, whatsoever things are honest, whatsoever things are just, whatsoever things are pure, whatsoever things are lovely, whatsoever things are of good report; if there be any virtue, and if there be any praise, think on these things," what a powerful enforcement is it to the exhortation, when the eloquence of a holy example, more persuasive than words, is felt in the heart of every hearer, saying, "Those things which ye have both learned, and received, and heard, and seen in me, do: and the God of peace shall be with you !"

The two parts of the clause under remark throw light on each other. The elder who lords it over his brethren, is not, cannot be, "an example" to the flock. He is the very reverse of an example. He exemplifies the temper which they ought most carefully to avoid; and, on the other hand, if the elder acts as an example to the flock, he cannot lord it over them.

The domineering elder cannot be an exemplary elder, and the exemplary elder cannot be a domineering elder. Nothing sits so gracefully on the ruler in the Christian church as kind condescension. Nothing is more unbecoming in him than overbearing haughtiness. The Master is the great model. "Ye call me Master and Lord: and ye say well; for so I am. If I then, your Lord and Master, have washed your feet, ye also ought to wash one another's feet. For I have given you an example, that ye should do as I have done to you. Verily, verily, I say unto you, The servant is not greater than his Lord; neither is he that is sent greater than he that sent him. If Christian elders know these things, happy will it be for themselves and for the churches if they do them."[31]

Such is the temper in which the duties of Christian elders should be performed, not reluctantly, but cheerfully; not mercenarily, but disinterestedly, from love to God and love to the brethren; not ambitiously, to display or establish superiority and rule, but humbly, for the purpose of setting an example of Christian obedience;[32] not to glorify themselves but to edify the brethren.

CHAPTER FOUR

OF THE MOTIVES TO THESE DUTIES

It still remains for us on this part of our subject to attend to the motives by which the Apostle urges Christian elders to discharge their duties in this manner. These motives are derived from considerations referring personally to the Apostle—" I exhort you; I who am a fellow-elder, a witness of the sufferings of Christ, and a partaker of the glory that shall be revealed;" from considerations referring to the church—it is "the flock of God," "God's heritage;" and from considerations referring to the office-bearers themselves—if they perform their duties in this way, "when the chief Shepherd appears, they shall receive a crown of glory, which fadeth not." Let us shortly endeavor to bring out the force of the motives arising from these three sources.

I. MOTIVES SUGGESTED BY THE APOSTLE'S REFERENCE TO HIMSELF

1. HE WAS ALSO AN ELDER

And first, let us consider the motives suggested by the Apostle's reference to himself. "The elders who are among you I exhort, who am also an elder, and a witness of the sufferings of Christ, and a partaker of the glory which shall be revealed." I exhort, says Peter; and who was he?" An Apostle of Jesus Christ," one of those so specially commissioned by Christ Jesus to act the part of ambassadors in his room, who is the great ambassador from God; as that when they exhorted it was "as though God did beseech men" by them; to whom he had said, "As the Father had sent me, so I send you; whatsoever ye bind on earth is bound in heaven; whatsoever ye loose on earth is loosed in heaven; he that receiveth you, receiveth me; and he that receiveth me, receiveth him that sent me; he that despiseth you, despiseth me: and he who despiseth me, despiseth him that sent me;" to whom the Son of Man, on sitting down on the throne of his glory, gave twelve thrones, on which they should sit and judge, rule the twelve tribes of the spiritual Israel; who, along with the inspired prophets, are the foundation on which the church is built, and whose names are represented in the Apocalypse as engraved on the jewelled foundations of the New Jerusalem. An exhortation from such a quarter was equivalent to a command. He that rejected the Apostles, "rejected not men, but God, who had given them his Spirit;" while they spoke as Apostles, Christ, and God in Christ, spoke by them. An apostolical exhortation is equivalent to a Divine command.[33]

The Apostles, though possessed of this authority, made no unnecessary display of it. It was generally acknowledged by the churches; and though they sometimes found it requisite to "command," as well as to exhort, in the name of the Lord Jesus, yet for the most part, "though they might be much bold in Christ" to enjoin that which was convenient, they "rather, for love's sake, besought" those whom they addressed. The injunction lost none of its intrinsic authority from the form it took; and, while more agreeable to him who gave, was not likely to be less influential on those to whom it was given. Peter not only uses the word exhort instead of command, but, instead of using the official appellation which was peculiar to the highest order of the church officers, Apostle, he employs that of "elder," which in its most general acceptation includes all church rulers. He does not take the name which distinguishes him from, but that which identifies him with, those whom he addresses.

Peter speaks of "the wisdom given to his beloved brother Paul;" and it is plain he himself had been made partaker of the same spirit of wisdom and of love. 'I am,' says the venerable Apostle, 'I am a co-presbyter, a fellow-elder. I know what it is to have a charge in the house of God. I have felt the responsibilities arising out of the command to feed the sheep, to feed the lambs of the great, good Shepherd. I know the duties of the Christian pastor; I know his difficulties; I know his temptations; I know his joys; I know his sorrows. I know the heart of the Christian elder. The exhortation comes from one who can, who does, thoroughly sympathize with you.'[34]

The kindly condescending address of the Apostle was calculated to give additional force to his exhortation, and its peculiar form is surely intended to teach elders, especially old elders, men who have been long in office in God's church, to use the influence which, if they have in any measure rightly discharged their duty, they must have acquired, in exhorting their fellow-elders, especially those younger than themselves, to diligence and fidelity in the duties of their common offices. "The duty of mutual exhorting, which lies on each Christian to another, is little known amongst the greater part; but surely pastors should be, as in other duties so in this, eminent and exemplary in their interchange and converse, saying often one to another, 'Oh, let us remember to what we are called, to how high and heavy a charge! to what holiness and diligence! How great the hazard of our miscarriage, and how great the reward of our fidelity!' whetting and sharpening one another by those weighty and holy considerations." It is peculiarly becoming in old Christian elders to say to their young brethren, especially when the exhortation is enforced by a protracted course of faithful services to Christ and his church, "Take heed to the ministry which ye have received of the Lord, that ye fulfill it." Such exhortations given in the right spirit seldom fail of doing good.

2. HE WAS A WITNESS OF THE SUFFERINGS OF CHRIST

To give further weight to his exhortation, the Apostle not only calls himself a fellow-elder, but "a witness of the sufferings of Christ." "The sufferings of Christ," which the ancient prophets are in the first chapter (v. 11) represented as witnesses of, as testifying about, are not, as I endeavored to show when explaining that part of the epistle, the personal sufferings of our Lord, but the "sufferings until Christ," or "the sufferings in reference to Christ," as the words literally signify, "the sufferings of the present time," to which for a season it is needful that Christians be exposed, as contrasted with the glory which is to follow, the salvation laid up in heaven, the grace to be brought to Christians at the revelation of our Lord Jesus. And some have supposed that the phrase "sufferings of Christ" has the same meaning here, and that the Apostle expresses the same sentiment as the Apostle Paul to the Thessalonians, when he says, "We told you before that we should suffer tribulation." There can be no doubt that Peter as well as Paul, when confirming the souls of the disciples, and exhorting them to continue in the faith, did testify, that "through much tribulation they must enter into the kingdom." [35] We find him doing so in this epistle, and this was in itself a good reason why he should exhort the office-bearers to a conscientious performance of their duties, for that, important at all times, becomes doubly so in a time of trial. But the expression here is not the same as that in the first chapter, and seems varied to show that it refers to

Christ's personal sufferings, and not to the sufferings of his body, the church, till he comes.

Of these sufferings Peter was "a witness." These words may signify that the sufferings of Christ were a principal subject of Peter's testimony as an Apostle. The Apostles, after they received power through the Holy Ghost coming upon them, were, according to their Master's appointment and prediction, "witnesses unto him both in Jerusalem, and in all Judea, and in Samaria, and unto the uttermost parts of the earth." And wherever they went, the cross was the great theme of their testimony, The Messiah they proclaimed was the crucified Messiah, "a stumbling-block to the Jews, foolishness to the Greeks; but to the called, whether Jew or Greek, the power of God, the wisdom of God." Peter, judging of the ministry from his discourses recorded in the Acts of the Apostles and in this epistle, had, as well as Paul, "determined to know nothing among his converts but Jesus Christ and him crucified." He, too, could say, "God forbid that I should glory, except in the cross of our Lord Jesus Christ, by which the world is crucified to me, and I to the world."[36]

It appears to me, however, more natural to understand the words, "a witness of the sufferings of Jesus Christ," in their most obvious sense as equivalent to, I saw Jesus Christ suffer. It is as if he had said, 'He who addresses you, and calls on you to be faithful to Christ, and to the church purchased by his blood, knows well how strong are his claims on you, how strong is his regard for them. With these eyes I have seen the Eternal Word, the Lord of Glory, a poor, destitute, afflicted, tormented, despised, dying, dead man. I heard his groans in Gethsemane. I saw his sweat, as it were great drops of lood, falling to the ground. I saw him betrayed by one of his disciples, Judas. I saw him deserted by them all. I saw him insulted and abused before the high priest. I saw how deeply he felt, and how tenderly he forgave, my base denial of him.' And as we can scarcely persuade ourselves that Peter and the other Apostles were not witnesses of the last scene of suffering, it is as if he said, 'I saw him affixed, like a felonious slave, to the cross. I heard the wail of agony, "My God, my God, why hast thou forsaken me!" I heard, though I then understood it not, the mysterious parting cry, "It is finished." Having witnessed all this, is it wonderful that His words who thus suffered for me, for you, for the flock committed to our care, that his words, Lovest thou me? feed my lambs; Lovest thou me? feed my sheep; Lovest thou me? feed my sheep—should be continually sounding in my ears, continually weighing on my heart, and that I should with deep earnestness exhort you to do that which he so impressively commanded me to do?'

"These, indeed, are things that give great weight to a man's words, make them powerful and pressing, 'a witness of the sufferings of Christ.' The Apostles had a singular advantage in this that they were eye-witnesses;[37] and Paul, who wanted that, had it supplied by a vision of Christ at his conversion. But certainly a spiritual view of Christ crucified is generally, I will not say absolutely, necessary to make a minister of Christ. It is certainly very requisite for the due witnessing of him, so to preach the gospel as one 'before whose eyes Jesus Christ had been evidently set forth crucified.' Men commonly read and hear, and may possibly preach, of the sufferings of Christ as a common story, and in that way it may a little move a man and wring tears from his eyes; but faith hath another kind of sight of them, and so works another kind of affection. By the eye of faith to see the only begotten Son of God, as stricken and smitten of God, bearing our sorrows and wounded for our transgressions; Jesus Christ, the righteous, reckoned among the unrighteous and malefactors; to see him stripped naked, and scourged, and buffeted, and reviled, and dying, and all for us; this is the thing that will bind upon us most strongly all the duties of Christianity, and of our callings; and best enable us according to our callings to bind them upon others." [38]

3. HE WAS A PARTAKER OF THE GLORY TO BE REVEALED

But still farther to add cogency to his exhortation, the Apostle styles himself "a partaker of the glory that shall be revealed." The glory here spoken of is obviously "the glory of Christ," a state of dignity and happiness contrasted with his suffering state. 'I am not only a witness of his sufferings, but a partaker of his glory, which is to be revealed.' Some have supposed that in these words there is a reference either to our Lord's transfiguration, or to his resurrection state, as if Peter had said, 'I witnessed and shared of his sufferings, and I have witnessed and shared too of his glory. I was "with him in the Holy Mount, when he received from God the Father honor and glory." I, though fearing, entered with him into the cloud of glory, from the midst of which came the voice, "This is my beloved Son, in whom I am well pleased." And I too companied with him after his resurrection, when God had "raised him from the dead and given him glory." I am one of those on whom he breathed and said, "Receive ye the Holy Ghost;" and of whom he also said, "The glory thou hast given me I have given them." That glory is as yet in this state veiled. It is "hid with Christ in God," but it will by and by be manifested.' [39]

It seems to me more natural to consider the glory here referred to as the glory of Christ in the celestial state. That glory at present is concealed, and shall continue so till the close of the present state of things. The glories of the holy of holies are hidden from this outer court of the temple by the veil of these visible heavens, through which our Lord has passed. But this veil shall by and by be rent asunder, and all the splendors of the inner sanctuary burst on the sight of an amazed world. "Christ, the life of his people, shall appear," be manifested to be what he is, and they his people shall be manifested with him in glory. The day of his manifestation as the Son of God shall be the day of their manifestation as the sons of God. He shall be "glorified in his saints, and admired in all them that believe;" and they shall be glorified in him, admired in him. [40]His glories shall be displayed; and it shall be made to appear that the glory his Father has given him he has given to his people.

Of this participation in the revealed glories of Christ, Peter was so persuaded in reference to himself, that he speaks of himself as already a partaker of the glory that shall be revealed. Having the spirit of faith, he was confident, "knowing that he that raised up the Lord Jesus would also raise up him by Jesus," and that he should be forever "with him where he is," beholding and sharing his glory, so far as the thing is possible, being "glorified together with him."[41] But the words are so chosen as, naturally enough, to convey, in addition to this thought, that he should be a partaker of the glory of Christ at the time of its revelation, the idea that even now, amid all the imperfections and sorrows of the present state, Peter considered himself as a partaker of the glory of Christ; that glory now concealed, but one day to be manifested. He considered himself as "planted together with Christ," not only "in the likeness of his death," but also "in the likeness of his resurrection;" as having fellowship with him not only in his death, but also in his life, "sitting with him, reigning with him, in the heavenly places;"[42] already a partaker, though in far inferior measure, of that holiness and happiness, in the enjoyment of the Divine favor and conformity to the Divine image, in the perfection of which Christ's glory consists. Peter was, and every Christian in the measure of his faith is, thus even here "a partaker of the glory which is to be revealed."

The bearing of this statement, as a motive on the Apostle's exhortation, is manifest when you look forward to its close, where he points to the crown of glory, which, when the Chief

Shepherd comes, that is, at the time of the revelation of his glory, shall be conferred on the faithful under-shepherds. The exhortation of a man, who, under the influence of the spirit of faith, believes, and therefore speaks, and who, when speaking of the future rewards of the faithful minister, speaks of something of which he has already the earnest, and of the full enjoyment of which he is completely assured, is plainly fitted to be peculiarly impressive and persuasive. It is as if he had said, "I speak what I do know. I testify what I have seen."

II. Motives from considerations referring to the church

Let us now look at the motives derived from considerations referring to the church. Feed the church; it is the flock of God. Superintend the church; it is the heritage of God.

1. It is the flock of God.

The church is the flock of God, and every true member of it is one of his sheep. This is one of the figurative expressions by which Jehovah's peculiar property in, and care for, ancient Israel is often expressed. "Ye, my flock, the flock of my pasture, are men, and I am your God, saith the Lord God." [43] Like most expressions of the kind, it is employed in an extended and elevated sense to describe the peculiar relation in which the true spiritual church stands to God. They are his peculiar property, separated from the rest of mankind, saved from destruction by the good Shepherd laying down his life for them; protected by his peculiar providence, and blessed with the tokens of his special love. The good Shepherd, who laid down his life to save them from destruction, took it again to complete their salvation: "He gathers the lambs in his arms, he carries them in his bosom;" "He feeds them, and causes them to lie down. He seeks that which was lost, and brings again that which was driven away; and binds that which was broken, and strengthens that which is sick." Hear what he himself says, "I give unto my sheep eternal life, and they shall never perish; neither shall any pluck them out of my hand. My Father, who gave them me, is greater than all; and none can pluck them out of my Father's hand." [44] Should not we count it a great honor, and feel it a most responsible trust, to have those who stand in so close a relation to God, in whom he takes so peculiar an interest, committed to our care? Should we not care for those for whom he cares? Should we not watch for those for whom his Son died?

2. It is God's heritage

Substantially the same ideas with regard to the church are suggested by its being termed God's heritage. The term here used has a reference to the manner in which the Israelites obtained their possessions, which were heritages transmitted from generation to generation. It is borrowed from the fact that these possessions were originally fixed by lot, so that lot and possession are often, in Scripture, convertible terms. Like the former figure, it is often used to express Jehovah's peculiar relation to Israel, "The Lord's portion is his people;

Israel is the lot of his inheritance;"[45] and both designations are transferred to the spiritual church under the new economy. Christians are called "the purchased possession," the peculiar property of God, "the chosen generation, the holy nation, the peculiar people." [46] To be employed to take care of his ancient people was a great honor. To be the king of Israel was greater honor than to be king of Egypt, Assyria, or Babylon. How far above all Pagan legislators stands Moses the servant of the Lord! How low the rank of heathen sages compared with that of Hebrew prophets! The most honorable and responsible situation man can occupy, is that of a teacher and ruler in that spiritual family of which God is the head, Jesus Christ is the elder brother, and holy angels the willing ministers. Should not God's most valued property be well cared for? Should not the education of his children be well attended to? Is there not great honor involved in the charge being entrusted to us? Must there not be high responsibility incurred by our undertaking it? Such seems the force of the motives derived from a reference to the church.

It is but right to remark, before leaving this particular, that the precise meaning of the expression, rendered "God's heritage," is somewhat doubtful. You will observe the word *God's* is in italics, which, as you know, indicates that there is no term answering to it in the original. The word is in the plural, the lots or possessions. Not lording it over "the lots."[47] The term lot or possession, in the singular, is applied to the church, as the lot or possession of Jehovah; but nowhere else in the plural. This has led some to suppose that it refers to the possessions, the property, of the church; not treating the church property, as if it were their own, as if they were the proprietors of it. There is no reason to think that at this early period the churches had anything like fixed property; and there is no proper contrast in this case between the two obviously antithetic clauses of the sentence. It is a much more probable opinion that considers the lots or possessions as referring to the separate flocks of different elders or elderships. Not lording it over the (or their) lots or possessions, the flocks allotted to them by the great Shepherd, but showing them an example. In this case, the motive folded up in the phrase is, You have had a specific work assigned you by the great Shepherd. Each has his appointed sphere of Tabor. Let the laborers see that their own vineyard be well kept, and their own flock be well shepherd-'ed. Yet a little while, and the great Husbandman will take account of his servants, and then woe to the unprofitable, double woe to the unfaithful servant.

III. Motives from considerations referring to the Office-bearers themselves

It only remains now that we attend a little to the motives derived from a reference to the office-bearers themselves. The words of the Apostle express much; they suggest more. They describe the reward of the faithful Christian elder; they dimly shadow forth the punishment of the unfaithful Christian elder.

1. The reward of the faithful Christian elder

The words describe the reward of the faithful Christian elder: "He shall receive a crown of glory, which fadeth not away, when the chief Shepherd shall appear." Jesus Christ is the chief Shepherd; he is the Shepherd of the sheep, the good Shepherd, the great Shepherd, the proprietor Shepherd, whose own the sheep are; the Shepherd of the shepherds as well as of the sheep. He is even now really present in his church. The faithful Witness did not lie when he said, "Lo, I am with you alway." "Where two or three are met in my name, I am in the midst of them." [48]

His presence, however, is spiritual, not bodily. The heavens have received him, and we see him no more. But when he disappeared, the most explicit declarations were given that he should re-appear. "I will come again," said he himself; "and receive you to myself, that where I am, there ye may be also." "This same Jesus," said the angels to the Apostles, when they stood gazing up towards heaven, in the clouds of which their Lord had just disappeared, "This same Jesus who is taken up from you into heaven, shall so come in like manner as ye have seen him go into heaven." [49] This re-appearance, which is to be a glorious manifestation of what he is, both essentially and officially, a revelation of his glory, is a leading subject of the apostolic testimony, and has been all along the great object of the church's hope. Their "blessed hope" is, and has all along been," the glorious appearing of Him who is the great God and their Savior." [50] The day of his coming is to be the day of their "gathering together to him."

When He shall come, he shall come in his character of the chief Shepherd, to collect his flock together, and to conduct them all in a body into the heavenly fold. One purpose of his coming shall be to take account of his under-shepherds, and to render to them according to their work. To the faithful, laborious servant, who has affectionately and wisely shepherded and superintended, fed and guided, the flock committed to him, not grudgingly, but cheerfully; not mercenarily, but disinterestedly; not ambitiously, seeking to be a lord, but humbly, striving to be an example; "he will then give a crown of glory which shall never fade."

The language is figurative, but the meaning is plain. He will visibly reward his faithful services, by bestowing on him a large measure of the highest kinds of happiness and honor of which his nature is capable; blessings which shall endure forever, and forever retain undiminished their power to satisfy their possessors. In what the peculiarity of the rewards of the faithful Christian elder shall consist, we can form but inadequate and indistinct ideas. There is much, however, to lead us to believe, that a portion, and probably no small portion of it, is to consist in witnessing the holy happiness of those to whose spiritual interests he ministered on earth; and to know most certainly, that to his labors and instrumentality their happiness has been owing. Such is the view which the Apostle's words naturally lead us to take, when he calls the Philippian Christians his "joy and his crown;" and when to the Thessalonians he says, "What is our hope, or joy, or crown of rejoicing? Are not even ye in the presence of our Lord Jesus Christ at his coming? for ye are our glory and our joy." [51]

The Christian pastor will, according to his measure, be admitted into the joy of his Lord, when he sees the travail of his soul, and is satisfied. This is an exceeding great, and a peculiarly appropriate reward; a reward which will be enjoyed just in proportion as the individual Christian pastor has been filled with the spirit of his office, and discharged its duties. What a high, what a holy satisfaction to know, that we have efficiently co-operated towards the accomplishment of the favorite purpose of Deity, to reconcile all things to himself by Jesus Christ; that we have been the means of saving souls from death, of covering multitudes of sins, of increasing the joys of angels, of ministering to the satisfaction of Him who loved us, and washed us from our sins in his own blood! What a reward!

To borrow the words of the holy Leighton, "It is a crown of glory, pure, unmixed glory, without any ingrediency of pride or sinful vanity, or any danger of it; and a crown that fadeth not, formed of such flowers that wither not; not a temporary garland of fading flowers, as all here are. Though made of flowers growing in a rich valley, their glorious beauty is fading; but this is fresh, and in perfect lustre, to all eternity. May they not well trample on base gain, and vain applause, that have this crown to look to? Joys of royal pomp, how soon do they vanish as a dream? But this day begins a triumph and a feast, that shall never either end or be wearied of. All things here, even the choicest pleasures, cloy, but satisfy not.

Those above shall always satisfy, but never cloy. What is to be refused in the way to this crown? All labor for it is sweet. And what is there here to be desired to stay our hearts, that we should not most willingly let go, to rest from our labors, and receive our crown? Was ever any man sad that the day of his coronation drew nigh? In that day when he on whose head are many crowns, shall bestow many crowns, there will be no envy, no jealousies; all kings, each having his own crown, and each rejoicing in the glory of another, and all in His, who that day shall be all in all."

2. THE DOOM OF THE UNFAITHFUL CHRISTIAN ELDER

These words of the Apostle, while they describe the final destiny of the faithful Christian pastor, naturally suggest the awful truth respecting the Christian elder who has not fed the flock of God, who has not superintended aright his heritage. What is to become of him who has done his work by constraint, not willingly, for filthy lucre, not of a willing mind, who has lorded it over God's heritage, and has not been an example to the flock; shall he be crowned? No; he has not "striven," or, at any rate, "not striven lawfully." The doom of the unprofitable, the doom of the unfaithful, servant will be his. Expelled from the family of God, he will be cast into outer darkness; there shall be weeping and gnashing of teeth. His portion is with the hypocrites, a class peculiarly hateful to him who desires truth in the inward part; with the perfidious, who have broken their engagements both to God and to man.

And it is his fit place; for the honor of God, the cause of truth, the interests of souls, were put into his hands; he accepted the trust, and basely betrayed them all. In the prison of hell, with "the basest, the lowermost, the most dejected, most underfoot and down-trodden vassals of perdition," [52] must he have his everlasting abode?" This pertaineth to him as the portion of his cup." What Christian elder can think of these things, can realize them to his mind, without having new nerve given to his resolution to be "faithful to him who has appointed him;" "faithful to death," that he may "obtain the crown of life," and escape the brand of everlasting shame and contempt; that he may be greeted with the invitation, "Well done, good and faithful servant," come up hither; instead of meeting the heart-withering denunciation, "Depart, depart, I never knew you." You called me, Lord; but I never considered you as my servant, for I knew you were not.

Thus have I brought to a close my illustrations of the first part of this paragraph, that part of it which refers to the duties of the office-bearers of the Christian church to those committed to their care. But ere proceeding farther, I would press on my own mind, and on the minds of my brethren in the eldership in this congregation, the solemn considerations which, in the illustration of this passage of Scripture, have been placed before us. Let us remember, that this word of exhortation is as really addressed to us, as it was to those to whom the epistle was originally written. Let us humble ourselves, under the consciousness how very imperfectly we have discharged the inestimably important duties of our most responsible situation. Let us cast ourselves on our Master's kindness, for the forgiveness of all that has been wanting and wrong in our official conduct; and while in our inmost hearts saying, "Who is sufficient for these things?" let us, undiscouraged though not unwarned by our former failures, cherish an overgrowing resoluteness of determination, by his grace, to be "steadfast and immovable, always abounding in the work of our Lord," assured that our labors shall not be in vain in the Lord.

Holy brethren, partakers of this high vocation, elders, suffer the words of exhortation from one who also is an elder. They shall be the words of the holy Apostles of our common Lord: "I charge you before God, and the Lord Jesus Christ, and the elect angels, that ye take heed to yourselves and to all the flock over which the Holy Ghost has made you overseers. Hold the mystery of faith in a pure conscience. Be examples to the believers in word, in conversation, in charity, in spirit, in faith, in purity. Let no man despise you. O men of God, flee pride, strife, evil surmisings, perverse disputings, and that love of money which is the root of all evil. Follow after righteousness, godliness, faith, love, patience, meekness. Fight the good fight of faith; lay hold on eternal life. Hold fast the form of sound words. Hold fast what you have attained; let no man take your crown. I give you charge in the sight of God, who quickeneth all things, and before Christ Jesus, who before Pontius Pilate witnessed a good confession, that you observe these things, without preferring one before another, doing nothing by partiality. Keep this commandment without spot, unrebukable, until the appearing of our Lord Jesus Christ: which in his times he shall show, who is the blessed and only Potentate, the King of kings, and the Lord of lords; who only hath immortality, dwelling in the light which no man can approach unto; whom no man hath seen, neither can see: to whom be honor and power everlasting. Amen." [53]

—PART TWO—

OF THE DUTIES OF THE MEMBERS OF THE CHRISTIAN CHURCH TO THEIR OFFICE-BEARERS

I go on now to call your attention to the view which the text gives us of the duties of the members of Christian churches towards their office-bearers. This is contained in the first clause of the fifth verse, "Likewise, ye younger, submit yourselves to the elder." Before proceeding farther, however, it will be proper that I endeavor to satisfy you that these words are, indeed, an injunction of the duties of church members to their office-bearers, and not, as many have supposed, of the duties of the young to the aged. Were we merely looking at the words, without taking into consideration the connection in which they are introduced, this last mode of viewing them would probably be that which would first occur to every reader; but it requires only a little reflection to see: first, that the connection by no means leads us to expect here an injunction of the duties of the young to the aged, and that the language by no means obliges us thus to understand it; and, secondly, that the connection does lead us to expect an injunction of the duties of the private members of the church, as contra-distinguished from the office-bearers; and, still farther, that while there is nothing in the language which is inconsistent with this mode of interpretation, there is something which cannot be satisfactorily explained on any other supposition.

There can be no doubt that the first four verses of the chapter refer to the duties of Christian office-bearers; and as little, that the injunction in the fifth verse has a close connection with the injunctions contained in these verses, a connection intimated by the connective particle "likewise;"[54] a word which seems to intimate that the duties enjoined are correlative, or, at any rate, belong to the same general family of duties. In enjoining domestic duties, after stating the duties of servants, the Apostle says, "*Likewise*, ye wives, be in subjection to your own husbands;" and after stating the duties of wives, he says, "*Likewise*, ye husbands, dwell with your wives according to knowledge, giving honor unto the wife, as unto the weaker vessel, and as being heirs together of the grace of life: that your prayers be not hindered."[55] The word certainly leads you to expect the injunction of some kindred, some ecclesiastical, duty, not the injunction of a duty belonging to an entirely different class.

It is the ordinary practice of the Apostles, a practice plainly dictated by the proprieties of the case, to enjoin the duties rising out of mutual relations in succession; thus, "Wives, submit yourselves to your own husbands; husbands, love your wives." "Children, obey your parents; fathers, provoke not your children to anger." "Servants, be obedient to them that are your masters; masters, do the same thing to them."[56] When, therefore, we meet with an injunction to elders to do their duty to a certain class clearly defined, and then find a certain class, not quite so clearly defined, called on to do their duty to elders, we naturally conclude that the objects of the first exhortations are the subjects of the second, and not some other class altogether.

Had the office-bearers been represented as spiritual fathers, and had the injunction run thus, "Fathers in Christ, carefully superintend and instruct the family of God committed to your care;" and been followed by the command, "Likewise, ye children, be submissive to the fathers;" would not every one at once have seen that, in the latter clause, it was not the duty of children to their parents that was enjoined, but that of spiritual children to their spiritual fathers—or in other words, of the members of the church to the office-bearers of the church?

It seems very unnatural, without a strong reason, to suppose the elders of the fifth verse to be a different class of men from the elders of the first verse;[57] and, if they are the same class, it seems strange that young persons alone should be called on to perform to them a duty which is owing to them by all to whom they stand in official relation. Besides, had the Apostle meant to enjoin the duties of the young to the old, he would have used some other word for the old than that which he had just used to express office. Still further, the duty enjoined is one due to all official elders, from their office; and not due to any old man, merely from his age. It is not submission, but respect, that is due from the young to the old. "Thou shalt rise up before the hoary head, and honor the face of the old man, and fear thy God: I am the Lord." [58]

We consider ourselves, then, as not only warranted, but shut up, to interpret "the younger," or the juniors here, as a general name for the ordinary church members, as contra-distinguished from their elders, in the same way as they are termed sheep, or a flock, when their office-bearers are termed shepherds; scholars, or disciples, when they are termed teachers; and as John the elder speaks of his converts as his children, "I have no greater joy than to hear that my children walk in truth." [59] I am not aware of the designation "younger" being used in any other part of the New Testament in the sense which it seems to bear here, though there is a passage where it is employed in a somewhat analogous way: "He that is greatest among you, let him be as the younger; and he that is chief, as he that doth serve." [60]

That the younger here are those who stand in some relation to the presbyters or elders just mentioned, is so evident, and its reference to the young in age is so unnatural, [61] that we find a number of commentators supposing that the term refers to the six inferior orders of clergy, [62] as they were called, after the simplicity of the primitive Christian polity was departed from; and that submission referred to their duties to the bishops. The use of such an expression for church members was natural in the primitive times, when their official elders were generally not young men, certainly not young Christians; it being matter of statute that the elders should not be novices, but tried men, old disciples; so that the great body of the church members were both naturally and spiritually their juniors. Indeed still, in ordinary cases, the great body of the members of a church are younger than their elders.

On the supposition that the younger, the juniors, are the private members of the church, the whole passage has a character of close connection and complete consistency. We have first the duties of the office-bearers; then the duty of the private members of the church to their office-bearers; and then the duty of all connected with the church, whether officers or private members, clearly stated and powerfully enforced. The duties enjoined are just the duties belonging to those who respectively occupy those ecclesiastical relations. On the other supposition all is disjointed. An injunction of the duties of Christian pastors is followed by an injunction of the duties of the young to the old; and this followed by an injunction of the duty which every man owes to every man; and the duties enjoined in the two last cases are not those which we expect; for, though the young are bound to respect the aged, they are not bound to submit to them; and, though every man is to be kind and just to every other man, every man is not bound to be subject to every man; though there is an important sense, in which every Christian man should be subject to every other Christian man; every church member to every other church member. Even Leighton, who follows the common mode of interpretation, acknowledges that the words have "some aspect to the relation of those that are under the discipline and government of the elders." The good archbishop was forgetful of the wise saying of Dr. Owen: "If Scripture have more meanings than one, it has no meaning at all." If the younger means the members of the church, it cannot mean the young properly so called.

Having thus ascertained that the injunction before us is an injunction to church members to perform their duty to their office-bearers, let us proceed now to inquire into the meaning of the injunction. What is the duty of church members to their office-bearers, as here described? The duty here enjoined is substantially the same as that enjoined by the Apostle Paul, in his Epistles to the Thessalonians and Hebrews. "We beseech you, brethren, to know, or acknowledge, them which labor among you, and are over you in the Lord, and admonish you; and to esteem them very highly in love for their work's sake." "Obey them that have the rule over you, and submit yourselves : for they watch for your souls, as they who must give account; that they may do it with joy, and not with grief: for that is unprofitable for you.'[63]

It is quite plain, from these passages, that obedience and submission are required from church members to their office-bearers. It is unhappily too certain, that much mischief has been done, and much good prevented, by church officers assuming a power and authority that do not belong to them, but to the one Lord, and encroaching on the liberties which every Christian possesses in unalienable right, by virtue of the gift of this one Lord; and by church members impiously permitting such an usurpation, and tamely submitting to such encroachments on their privileges. But it is just as unhappily notorious, that much mischief has been done, and much good prevented, in the Christian church, by anarchy as well as tyranny: by church members refusing to obey them that are over them in the Lord, and by church officers allowing themselves to be denuded of the authority with which their Master has clothed them, and without the exercise of which the great and salutary ends of their office cannot be gained.

A Christian church is a very free society; but they mistake the matter who consider it as a democracy. It is a monarchy, administered by inferior magistrates, chosen by their fellow-subjects, who are to execute the King's laws, being guided solely by his word, and neither by their own judgment or caprice, nor by the opinions and will of those whom they govern. Christ is the Lord, and he administers his government by officers appointed according to his ordinance, and regulated by his laws. It is of great importance, both to the office-bearers and private members of a Christian church, that they have distinct scriptural views on this subject, that the former may not exact what they have no right to, and that the latter may not refuse what, by the law of Christ, they are bound to give.

It is an elementary principle in the Christian polity, that the office-bearers of every Christian church should be chosen by the members of that church. No man should become an office-bearer in the Christian church, but thus by the suffrage of his brethren: and every individual, in joining a Christian church which has office-bearers, by doing so chooses them as his ecclesiastical superiors. Pastors and teachers are Christ's gifts.[64] The Holy Ghost constitutes all true ecclesiastical overseers;[65] but he does this, not by miraculous interposition, but by endowing them with the suitable qualifications, and inclining their brethren to call them to the exercise of these gifts. The primitive church elected their own officers. The Apostles ordained them, but those ordained by them were chosen by the brethren.[66]

The power of election was with them, and continued to be so, till the church became so corrupted as scarcely to deserve the name. So important is this consideration, in my apprehension, that I could not plead for obedience or submission as an ecclesiastical duty from Christian men in their social capacity, to a person imposed on them from without, either by civil or ecclesiastical authority. Non-intrusion is the fundamental principle of the administrative polity of the Christian church. Where a man, claiming rightly or wrongly the character of an elder in Christ's church, is not chosen explicitly or implicitly by me to be over me in the Lord, I am not bound to submit to him as my pastor.

Even to those elders whom the members of a church have explicitly or implicitly chosen to be their elders, the obedience due is obedience within certain clearly defined limits. It is only in the discharge of the duties of their office that they are to be submitted to; and even in the discharge of these duties, they are to be submitted to only as far as they administer the law of the one Lord. It is not to the arbitrary will of your elders that you are bound to submit. It is to them declaring and executing the will of Christ.4 "Pastors" (that is, elders) says Mr. Fuller, "are that to a church which the executive powers or magistrates of a free country are to the people at large; the organs of the law. Submission to them is submission to the law." If elders teach doctrine inconsistent with the doctrine of Christ, or enjoin anything inconsistent with his law, they are not to be submitted to, but on the contrary opposed; opposed to the face, for they are to be blamed. But when the Christian eldership keep themselves within the proper bounds of their office, it is the duty of all private members of the society to submit to and obey them; and they cannot do otherwise without disturbing the peace of the society, interfering with the edification both of themselves and of their fellow church members, and drawing down upon themselves that disapprobation with which the one Lord, who is the Author of order and not confusion, must regard all who resist his ordinances.

The truth on the subject of church authority has never been better stated than by the learned and judicious Dr. Owen: "The obedience due to church rulers is not a blind, implicit obedience. A pretense hereof has been abused to the ruin of the souls of men; but there is nothing more contrary to the whole nature of gospel obedience, which is our reasonable service. It has respect unto them in their office only, and while they teach the things which the Lord Christ hath appointed them to teach; when they depart from these, there is neither obedience nor submission due to them. Wherefore, in the performance of these duties, there is supposed a judgment to be made of what is enjoined or taught by the word of God. Our obedience unto them must be obedience to God. On these suppositions their word is to be obeyed, and their rule submitted to, not only because they are true and right materially, but also because they are theirs, and conveyed from them unto us by Divine institution."[67]

Keeping these general remarks in view, let us proceed to consider a little more particularly what is included in that submissive obedience which the Christian people, according to the law of the Lord, owe to the office-bearers whom they themselves have chosen. And here, with a reference to the view taken of the official duties of the eldership in a former part of this discourse, I shall show, in succession, how the members of the church are to submit themselves to the elders teaching, and to the elders superintending or governing. But before entering on this illustration, I have to solicit your attention, for a moment, to two things which may be considered as necessary prerequisites, in order to any individual rightly discharging his duty to the eldership, in either of these aspects. These are, first, a reverence for church government as an ordinance of Christ; and secondly, a respect for the persons who, in the church of which the individual is a member, are invested with office.

I. Preliminary requisites to the discharge of the duty of subjection to Elders

1. Conviction of the Divine authority of church order

To fit a man for the right discharge of the duty here enjoined, it is not necessary that he should be persuaded that every arrangement in the church with which he is connected is of Divine authority; but it is of great importance that he should be persuaded that the Christian church is a divine, not a human, institution; and that its office-bearers, properly chosen, are authorized by its Divine Head to execute his laws, and administer his ordinances. Without such a conviction, ecclesiastical obedience, as a religious duty, is impossible. The individual may comply with the arrangements as expedient, but he must feel himself at liberty, whenever he thinks them inexpedient, which is nearly equivalent to whenever he feels them to be inconvenient, to decline compliance with them. A Christian church is a voluntary society, inasmuch as no man can lawfully be compelled either to enter into its fellowship or to continue in it; but it is not a voluntary society, either in the sense that a Christian man can, without impropriety, continue unconnected with it; or, having connected himself with it, is not bound to submit to the laws ot its Lord and King, administered by office-bearers appointed according to his revealed will.

A great deal of the insubordination which prevails in Christian churches originates in the want of just views and settled convictions on this point. It is certainly true of ecclesiastical government in a higher sense than of civil government, that it is "of God;" and that "he who resists it," in the performance of its legitimate functions, "resists the ordinance of God, and receives to himself condemnation;" and this holds good, whatever form ecclesiastical government may assume, provided only the rights of Jesus Christ as the Head of the Church, and the privileges of his people, the members of it, are secured.

2. PERSONAL RESPECT FOR THOSE INVESTED WITH OFFICE

Inferior in importance to this, but only inferior to it, is the second prerequisite to the right discharge of the duty of submission or obedience to church officers: A personal respect for the individuals invested with office. To discharge the duties of civil obedience without this, is difficult. Without this, to discharge the duties of ecclesiastical obedience is impossible. No man ought to become a member of a church where the office-bearers, as a body, do not command his respect for their personal qualifications. He sports with his own edification if he does so. Nor ought he to continue a member of a church, where, as a body, they forfeit their claims on his respect. This is obvious; for how, in this case, can he have Christian fellowship with them?

In churches, in any good measure rightly constituted, the office-bearers are likely to be men worthy of esteem for their own sake, as well as for their work's sake. If they are not it must reflect much discredit on those who placed them in a situation so prominent and so responsible; a station which men of low Christian attainments, and doubtful spiritual character, cannot occupy without dishonor to Christianity, and injury to the edification of the church. This consideration ought to have a powerful effect on the minds of church members in electing office-bearers, and of Christians fixing on a particular religious society with which permanently to connect themselves. They ought to see to it that the elders of the church they belong to, be such men as that nothing in their private character and deportment shall throw obstacles in the way of the discharge of the duty due to them as public officers; but that, on the contrary, the respect which they cannot but feel for their worth as Christian brethren, shall make it a very easy thing to render to them the honor and submission due to them as Christian elders.

II. Subjection to the Elders as Teachers

Let me now a little more particularly consider what this honor and submission is, in reference to the two great departments of the elders' official duty, explained in a former part of this discourse: Teaching and superintendence. And first, of the submission which church members owe to their elders as teachers. Now, church members are certainly not bound to believe everything their elders teach, nor to do everything they enjoin; nay, they are not bound to believe anything they teach, merely because they teach it; to do anything they enjoin, merely because they enjoin it. But they are bound to submit to their teaching, both by regularly and conscientiously waiting on their instructions, and by receiving these instructions in the candid, humble spirit of discipleship.

Attendance on, and attention to, his teaching, is what every Christian teaching elder is entitled to from those under his care. It is the duty of the Christian teacher to "wait on his teaching."[68] The Christian teaching elder, who, without a very sufficient reason, is not in his own place when the church assembles to observe the ordinances of Christ, among which attention to the doctrine of the Apostles is one of the most important, is in fault. He ought to be there, prepared to expound and enforce the doctrine and law of the Lord, like a householder with a well-furnished store, out of which he is ready to distribute things new and old, "to give to each of the household his portion in due season." But the same authority which requires the elders to be present to teach, requires the brethren to be present to be taught. The pulpit must not only be filled, but in every case where there is not a sufficient reason for absence, filled by its proper occupant; and so ought the pew. Regular attendance on the public instructions of the teaching elders is the fundamental part of submission to them. If you do not hear your own elders, how can you be taught by them so as to be "obedient to them in the Lord?" And it is of importance that there should be attendance at the hour as well as on the day of public instruction. Punctuality as well as regularity should be attended to. It should be said of every Christian assembly as of Peter's congregation in the house of Cornelius, when the minister rises to address them,

"They are *all* present before God, to hear all things that are commanded him of God."[69]

The remark respecting attendance on the instruction of the elders, applies not only to their public teaching, but also to their ministrations from house to house. It is obviously the duty of the church members, so far as it is practicable, to afford the elders an opportunity of giving them those instructions more appropriate to their individual character and circumstances, which it would be unsuitable to communicate in public addresses.

But there must be attention as well as attendance; church members must show their submission to their elders' teaching, not only by a regular personal waiting on their instructions, but also by giving them the ready attention and the respectful consideration they deserve. They are to listen, and to listen not in the temper of captious critics, but of humble docile disciples; as persons who are come to learn the doctrine and law of the Lord, and who consider the teaching eldership as his appointed ordinance for bringing and keeping this doctrine and law before their mind. It is one of the many advantages of a stated ministry, that they who have placed themselves under it, are in a great measure freed from temptation to indulge in that critical mode of hearing, in which the hearer acts the part rather of the judge than of the disciple; seeking to form an opinion respecting the powers of the mind, the orthodoxy of the doctrine, or the qualities of the style and manner of the preacher, rather than to derive spiritual improvement. The church member, in listening to the teacher whom he has chosen, with whose character and qualifications he is satisfied, with whose style and manner he is familiar, is, no doubt, to judge of the accordance of what he hears with the Divine infallible exhibition of the doctrine and law of Christ, like one whose spiritual senses are exercised to discern good and evil; but he is to come, expecting to hear nothing reprehensible, disposed to give a candid consideration to everything that is said, anxious to hear what God the Lord will say to him, and expecting to hear this through the medium of his own elders, the instructors of his own unbiased choice, the divinely-appointed organs of instruction, and determined to "receive with meekness the word," which, if "engrafted" into him, will indeed "save his soul."

Instead of taking offence when the elder in teaching comes very close to his conscience, the church member should readily and thankfully receive "the reproof which gives "wisdom;" and, instead of rising in inward rebellion against the preacher, should accept the warning and rebuke which through his instrumentality is administered by his Master and ours. The church member who treats the instructions of the elders in an opposite spirit, violates the law in the text, forgets his place in the body of Christ, and throws almost invincible obstacles in the way of their usefulness, and his own edification. It is a just observation of Mr. Fuller, "If men attend preaching merely as judges of its orthodoxy, they will receive no advantage to themselves, and may do much harm to others. It is the humble Christian who hears that he may be instructed, corrected, and quickened in the ways of God, who will obtain that consolation which the gospel affords."

III. Submission to the elders as superintendents

It only remains now that we say a few words on the duty of submission due by church members to their elders as superintendents, as those who are "over them in the Lord," who "have the oversight of them," who "have the rule over them." And here I will, first, attend to the submission which is due to the eldership in their corporate capacity, and then to that which is due to individual elders when performing their duties as superintendents.

1. Submission to the eldership as a body

Submission to the eldership as a body, or to the session, as we call that body, has a reference to the two great functions that body has to perform: the preservation of external order in the society, and the exercise of spiritual discipline in the society. It is plain that in such a society as a Christian church, there are certain arrangements with respect to the time and place of meeting, and the order and minor circumstances of the services, that must be made and attended to. It belongs to the eldership to make such regulations, and it is the duty of the members of the church to observe them. These arrangements may not in every case seem to individual members to be the best; they may not be the best. It is quite right in private members to suggest to the elders what they think would be an improvement; but it is for the elders to judge of such things; and their judgment, in every case where conscience is not concerned, should be submitted to. If this be not attended to, there can be no such thing as order in a church.

The other form of submission to the eldership, submission to them as the administrators of the discipline of the society, requires somewhat more extended illustration. The admission of members into the body, the dealing with such members as have violated the laws of the society, and the exclusion of obstinate offenders from the society, are important official duties of the eldership. In the right discharge of these functions, the members of the society have a deep interest, and every member of the church should show that he is aware of this. The province of the members is not, however, directly to do these things; but to furnish, where they have it in their power, the means to the eldership to do them to the best advantage. It is their duty, when they are aware that individuals are applying for admission into the society, to give their elders any information which may help them to a right decision in a question of vital importance to the body; and in the same way, when offences occur, after having used in vain the means appointed by our Lord (Matt, xviii.) for having them removed privately, to bring the subject before the assembly of the eldership, and to give them all the assistance in their power to have it properly disposed of. Every member of a church is bound "to look diligently lest any fellow church member fail of the grace of God; lest any root of bitterness springing up trouble the body, and many be defiled."[70]

In the decisions of the eldership, as to admission, discipline, and exclusion, it is the duty of the members of the church to acquiesce, except in cases where they have satisfactory evidence that the law of Christ has not been rightly administered; and even where they may suppose that this has been the case, they are not to take it on them to judge and condemn those whom they themselves have elected to judge in such matters; far less are they to blazon their view of the matter before the church, least of all before the world. They are respectfully to remonstrate with the eldership, and, if they cannot obtain satisfaction, they are to apply to those larger associations of elders, which, under the name of presbyteries and synods, our church polity, in harmony, as we think, with the great leading principles of order laid down in the New Testament, provides; and if even then they cannot obtain satisfaction, if the matter is of such importance as to require it, after giving testimony against what they consider as a violation of the law of Christ, they should peaceably retire from the society. For private members of the church to counterwork the eldership in the legitimate discharge of their functions; to attempt, by producing popular commotions, to overawe their deliberations, or interfere with and overthrow their judgments, is plainly inconsistent with everything like good order, and directly opposed to that submission here enjoined by the supreme authority in the church.

Before leaving this part of the subject, I must say a word or two as to the duty of submission which a member of the church owes to the eldership when he himself unhappily becomes a subject of discipline. Such a person, though innocent, may, through mistake, or even through malignity, be regularly brought before the session as an accused person. In such circumstances, the individual concerned is not to refuse to submit the case to trial. He is not to behave as if he thought the eldership were acting an unkind part to him, in doing what they are imperatively bound to do, to examine every question connected with the purity of the body, regularly brought before them; he is to furnish them with the means of vindicating his character and that of the body, if he has been unjustly accused; and if he have really committed a fault, he is readily to acknowledge it, not carping at every mistake that may have been committed either by his accusers or judges, but by confession, penitence, and reformation, putting it in the power of the elders, with as little delay as possible, to restore him.

It is a very hazardous thing for offending members of a church not to submit themselves to their elders, when, in the impartial administration of the wise and benignant law of Christ, they are endeavoring to heal their backslidings, and wipe off the stain their conduct has cast on the worthy name, and remove the stumbling-block it has cast before both the church and the world. It is no light matter to set at naught the authority of an assembly of elders met in the name of Christ, and intelligently and honestly administering his laws. A deeper solemnity hangs over such an assembly, however humble in worldly ranks may be its members, than over the highest court which refers merely to the affairs of this world. He that despiseth them, despiseth their Lord; and he who despiseth him, despiseth also him who sent him.

2. SUBMISSION TO THE ELDERS AS INDIVIDUALS

A very few remarks on the duty of submission due from the church members to the individual elder, in discharging his function of superintendence, shall conclude these discussions. It is the duty of the elder to watch for the souls of those placed under his more immediate superintendence, to see that those duties on which their church membership is suspended be carefully performed. I refer to such duties as attendance on public worship, the religious government and education of their families, the maintenance of family worship, etc. It is also their duty to see that they be generally acting as becometh saints; walking so as to please God, and adorning the doctrine of God our Savior in all things.

To enable himself to perform these duties, the elder must seek a more intimate acquaintance with those under his care, than the mere common interchange of society can give; and must make inquiries which, from a stranger, would be justly counted intrusive and impertinent. The inquiries of the elder should be kindly taken, as originating in a desire to preserve a good conscience to himself, and to promote the highest interests both of the individual and of the society. And when he finds it necessary to exhort, and warn, and even rebuke privately, all this proceeding from a regard to Christ's law, and being, indeed, but an execution of it, is to be met in a becoming spirit, not submitted to as a hardship, but received as a privilege. The proper discharge of these private duties of the elder, and the meeting them in a right spirit, would mightily promote the edification of the body, and most happily lighten the disciplinary labors of the eldership.

"It has long appeared to me," says that wise and good man Andrew Fuller, "that there are some species of faults in church members, which are not proper objects of church censure, but of private pastoral admonition" by the elders; "such as spiritual declension, hesitation on important truth, occasional neglect of religious duties, worldly anxieties, and the early approaches to any evil course. A faithful elder,[71] with an eye of watchful tenderness, will perceive the first symptoms of spiritual disorder, and by a timely hint will counteract its operations." The church member may be aware that this is very self-denying work to the elder, who would much rather visit him with the smile of affectionate congratulation than with a countenance which says, 'My child, I stand in doubt of you.' And they ought not to render that disagreeable but important part of his work more disagreeable, by manifesting an irritable and resentful disposition, but receive the warning and the reproof which Christian love dictates, and which Christian law requires, with candor, and even with gratitude. "Correction may be grievous to him that forsaketh the way, but he that hateth reproof shall die."[72]

Such is a short view of the duty of church members to their office-bearers, as here enjoined by the Apostle. It is indeed what Archbishop Leighton terms it, just "the obedience due to the discipline of God's house. This is all we plead for on this point. And know, if you refuse it, and despise the ordinance of God, he will resent the indignity as done to him. And oh, that all that have that charge of his house upon them would mind his interest wholly, and not rise in conceit of their power, but wholly employ and improve it for their Lord and Master; and look on no respect to themselves, as for themselves desirable, but only so far as is needful for the profitable discharge and advances of the work in their hands. What are the differences and regards of men? How empty a vapor! and whatsoever it is, nothing is Tost by single and entire love of our Lord's glory, and total aiming at that. Them that honor him He will honor, and those that despise Him shall be despised."

I shall conclude this part of the subject by briefly illustrating the argument by which the Apostle, in the Epistle to the Hebrews, enforces compliance with an injunction of parallel meaning. "Obey them that have the rule over you, and submit yourselves; for they watch for your souls, as they that must give account; that they may do it with joy, and not with grief: for that is unprofitable for you."[73] Think of the work in which they are engaged; think of the character which they bear in performing it; think of the effect which your obedience or disobedience will have on the manner in which this work will be performed; and think of the influence which the manner in which their work is performed will have on your own interests.

Think of the work of your elders. They watch, they watch for you, they watch for your souls. They watch; their work requires constant solicitude; they must be ever on the alert, to observe danger and to prevent evil. They watch for you. Your best interests are the object of their solicitude. They are not watching for their own emolument or fame, but for your happiness. Others are watching against you; they are watching for you. Satan is watching you as a wolf the sheepfold, to steal and to destroy. Your elders watch, as faithful shepherds, to protect and save you. The world is watching you with a malignant eye, waiting for your halting. Your elders are watching, with the solicitude of parents, to keep you from falling. They watch for your souls—for that which is, of all you possess, most precious. Surely those who are benevolently engaged in a work so full of solicitude, and labor to promote your highest interests should not be counteracted by you, as they will be if you be not subject to them in the Lord.

Then think of the character they bear in doing this work. They watch as they who must give account. They are commissioned and responsible. What they do, they do by the authority of him who has appointed them. Do not resist them in their proper work, as you would not offend Him; and remembering that they must give account to him, recollecting what a stake they have in the matter, do not wonder that they should hazard offending you by the discharge of their duty, rather than run the risk of being ashamed before him at his coming, as they must be if they act not the part of faithful watchmen.

Consider, still further, the effect which your submission, or non-submission, is likely to have on their discharge of their work. If you do not submit yourselves, they will perform their work with grief. There are few bitterer sorrows than that of a faithful elder, laboring among a people who counteract his attempts to promote their spiritual improvement. Even Moses, one of "the elders, who by faith received a good report," when the Israelitish people were disobedient and rebellious, was tempted to wish that God would kill him out of hand rather than continue to cause him to see his wretchedness. [74] Slothful, selfish, cold-hearted, cavilling, conceited, contentious congregations, have broken the spirit of many a faithful minister of Christ, and made him go mourning to the grave.

And if you do submit yourselves, they will perform their work with joy. They will have a holy satisfaction in it. Their work will be their reward. Their hearts will be lifted up in the ways of the Lord. The joy of the Lord will be their strength. All good Christian elders can say with John the elder, "We have no greater joy than to see our children walk in truth."

And then, finally, think of the influence which the manner in which the work is performed will have on your own interests. If it is performed with grief, that will be unprofitable for you. The labors of a disheartened spiritual teacher or superintendent are not likely to be effective. Even where there is the highest degree of spiritual holy principle, the hands will wax feeble when the heart is discouraged; and the blessing of the great Master is not likely to be imparted when his commands are disregarded, and his servants misused. On the other hand, if your elder's work is performed with joy, it will be profitable to you. He will be enabled to do all his work in the most satisfactory way. His best affections will be strongly drawn out to those who rightly estimate his labors, and show a regard to the law of the Lord; and he will pray for you, and preach to you with double fervor and impressiveness. Seeing of the travail of his Master's soul, and of his own, he will be satisfied; and he will become more and more desirous that those in whom the good work is going forward, under his instrumentality, may grow in all holy attainments; he will become ingenious in devising, and unwearied in executing, plans for their spiritual improvement; and the great Head of the church, regarding with a benignant smile the affectionate laborious eldership, and the docile obedient church, will pour out on them in rich abundance of the selectest influences of his grace, and bless them, and make them blessings. Happy elders! Happy church! In their experience is verified the ancient oracle, "Then shall thy light break forth as the morning, and thine health shall spring forth speedily; and thy righteousness shall go before thee; the glory of the Lord shall be thy reward. And the Lord shall guide thee continually, and satisfy thy soul in drought, and make fat thy bones: and thou shalt be like a watered garden, and like a spring of water, whose waters fail not."[75]

PART THREE

OF THE DUTY WHICH ALL IN A CHRISTIAN CHURCH OWE TO EACH OTHER, "MUTUAL SUBJECTION"

There still remains to be considered the duty which all in a Christian church, whether office-bearers or private members, owe to each other, as stated by the Apostle in these words, "Yea, all of you be subject one to another, and be clothed with humility: for God resisteth the proud, and giveth grace to the humble."

It has been supposed by some interpreters, that these words are not to be considered as having any particular reference to Christians in their ecclesiastical relations, but as an injunction referring to all the relations of human life; and that the subjection one to another required, is either that mutual kindly consideration of each other's interests, and that readiness to submit to inconvenience to promote these interests, which is required by the law, "Whatsoever ye would that men should do to you, do also to them," and which is equally due in all the relations of society, from all to all; or that the Apostle meant to intimate, that not only in the ecclesiastical relation, but in all the relations of life, subjection to superiors is a Christian duty; that not only is the church member to be subject to the church ruler, but the member of the state to the state ruler, the member of the family to the family ruler; the wife to the husband, the child to the parent, the servant to the master; that, in one word, wherever the relation of inferior and superior is established by God, there the duty of subjection finds place, as in Ephesians v. 21, where the general command, "Submit yourselves to one another," is followed and illustrated by the particular injunctions, 'Wives, submit yourselves to your husbands; children, obey your parents; servants be obedient to your masters.' Either of these important moral truths might, without violence, be brought out of the words before us, viewed by themselves; but considered as a part of a closely connected paragraph, there can be no reasonable doubt, that the term "all of you," refers to the elders and to the juniors just mentioned, the office-bearers and members of the church; and that the duty enjoined is a duty equally owing by the elders to each other, by the members to each other, and by the elders and members to each other.

It may be of use in enabling you to perceive the precise import and bearing of the Apostle's words, to remark, that their literal rendering is, "But let all of you, being subject one to another, be clothed with humility; for God resisteth the proud, but he giveth grace to the humble." As if he had said, 'While it is the duty of church officers to exercise the rule with which Christ has invested them, and for church members to yield the obedience which Christ has enjoined on them, there is a kind of mutual subjection which all church members owe to all church members; which all church officers owe to all church officers; ay, which all church officers owe to all church members; in order to the discharge of which, it is necessary to cherish and display that humility which is in a remarkable degree the object of the Divine approbation.' There are obviously three topics which the Apostle's words bring before the mind, and which must be successively considered. 1. The duty which all connected with the Christian church, whether as office-bearers or members, owe to each other—mutual subjection. 2. The means which are necessary to the discharge of this duty—the being clothed with, that is, the cherishing and manifesting humility; and, 3. The motive urging the use of this means, its being the object of the peculiar approbation of God—" God resisteth the proud, and giveth grace to the humble."

OF THE MUTUAL SUBJECTION WHICH ALL IN A CHRISTIAN CHURCH OWE TO EACH OTHER

I. WHAT THIS DOES NOT IMPLY

Let us first, then, inquire, what is that Mutual Subjection which the Apostle here enjoins on all Christians, whether office-bearers or private members. It is so plain as scarcely to require to be noticed, that the subjection here required is by no means the same thing, though expressed by the same word, as the submission which, in the preceding clause, the juniors are enjoined to yield to the elders, the church members to the church rulers. It is obvious that church members are not bound to submit, to be subject, to their fellow church members, as they are to their elders; still less, if possible, can elders be bound to submit or be subject to the members, as the members are to be to them. This is obviously impossible; and to attempt it, were just, in other words, to annul church government, and to introduce all the disorders of ecclesiastical anarchy.

Nor does the command before us enjoin anything that in any degree involves in it a compromise of conscientious conviction respecting truth or duty. Christians must not submit to each other by taking each other's conscience as a guide in matters of faith or duty. Every man must give account of *himself* to God; and, so far as fellow-men or fellow-Christians are concerned, every man must think, inquire, judge, act, for himself. "One is our Master, even Christ."

The Christian elder must not, in teaching or administering the law of Christ, fashion his conduct in subservience to the views and wishes of those committed to his care. He must speak what he knows to be true, because it is Christ's doctrine, whatever they may think of it. He must do what he knows to be right, because it is Christ's law, whatever they may think of it. He must not, in this way, be a servant of men, even of Christian men. Were he to serve men in this way he could not be a servant of Christ. Were he to serve them in this way he would disserve them in a more important way.

No Christian man must submit, in matters of conscience, to be led by another, to avow or conceal what he wishes him to avow or conceal; to do or refrain from doing, what he wishes him to do or refrain from doing. Instead of being thus subject to one another, when any such submission is sought, either on the part of fellow church members, or of church office-bearers, we are not to give subjection to such usurpation, "no, not for an hour." Our submission to one another is to be submission "in the fear of God."

II. WHAT THIS DOES IMPLY

The mutual subjection referred to obviously implies a distinct recognition of, and a sacred regard to, our mutual rights as Christians and church members. Every encroachment by elders on the rights of church members, every encroachment by church members on the rights of their elders, every encroachment by church members, either individually or collectively, on each other's rights—and there has been a great deal too much of all these kinds of encroachment in the history of Christianity—is inconsistent with this mutual subjection. Every Christian man, official or unofficial, is to be yielded to, submitted to, in the exercise of his legitimate rights. This is most reasonable; it is absolutely necessary to the peace of the society; and, if carefully and uniformly attended to, would go very far to secure that peace.

This regard for mutual rights must be connected with a just, and, because a just, a high estimate of the honor due to Christians as Christians. No man will ever perform well the duties of civil life who has not learned to "honor all men;" to honor man as man, and to see that the circumstances which distinguish one man from another are as nothing when compared with those which distinguish all men from the lower creation. In like manner, the higher a Christian estimates those privileges which are possessed by all Christians as Christians, and those spiritual characteristics which belong to every Christian, and which can belong to none but a Christian, the better will he be prepared to perform the duty here enjoined. Every Christian, just because he is a Christian, in relation and character a child of God, will be an object of his respectful affection; and he will find it impossible intentionally to treat him unjustly, contemptuously, or unkindly.

The disposition to mutual submission is greatly strengthened by that generous appreciation of the personal Christian excellences of those with whom we are associated in church fellowship, to which Christian principle naturally leads. Christians should be eagle-eyed towards each other's good qualities, "in honor preferring one another," each "esteeming others better than themselves."[76] When this state of mind prevails, "being subject to one another" follows as a matter of course. There is a disposition to oblige, a backwardness to occasion pain. While there is a mutual teaching, admonition, and exhortation, there is a mutual submission to instruction, admonition, and exhortation. And while a brother does not so hate his brother in his heart as to suffer sin on him, his brother reproved says by his conduct "Let the righteous smite me, it shall be a kindness; and let him reprove me, it shall be an excellent oil, which shall not break my head." Even Archippus, the office-bearer, will be subject to him, whether an official or only a Christian brother, who in the right spirit says to him, "Take heed to the ministry which thou hast received of the Lord, to fulfill it."[77] There is a kindly yielding to each other in matters which do not involve conscience; and there is a serving one another in love, a readiness to submit to labor and inconvenience to promote one another's true happiness. Instead of insisting on having everything our own way, we have a satisfaction in pleasing, every one his neighbor, to his edification. We not only bear with the infirmities of our brethren: We bear their infirmities, not pleasing ourselves. We "forbear one another in love," and "seek not every man his own, but every man his neighbor's wealth."[78]

Such was the temper and conduct of the great Apostle of the Gentiles. Though free from all, he became the servant of all. He most willingly both spent, and was spent, to promote the welfare of his brethren; and declares that he would neither eat flesh nor drink wine, while the world stood, if by this means his brother were likely to be offended, or made weak. "Who was weak, and he was not weak; who was offended, while he did not burn. To the weak he became as weak, that he might gain the weak. To the Jew he became as a Jew, that he might gain the Jew; to them who were under the law, as under the law, that he might gain them who were under the law; to them who were without law, as without law, not being without law to God, but under the law to Christ, that he might gain them without law. He became all things to all men, that he might gain some."[79] Nor was this disposition in him confined to fellow Christians; he was willing to be thus subject to every man, if that might but promote his happiness, secure his salvation.

Such was the temper and conduct of the great Apostle's infinitely greater Lord and Master, and ours. He, though "Lord of all," became "the servant of all." Amid his disciples, he was as "one who served." "The Son of man," said he, and the whole of his life was an illustration of the saying, "The Son of man came not to be ministered unto, but to minister, and give his life a ransom for many."[80] Never was the lesson here given by the Apostle so strikingly taught, and so powerfully recommended, as in the conduct of our Lord in that memorable night in which he was betrayed, of which we have so touching a narrative in the evangelical history. "Now, before the feast of the passover, when Jesus knew that his hour was come, that he should depart out of this world unto the Father, having loved his own which were in the world, he loved them to the end. And there was a strife among the disciples, which of them should be accounted the greatest. And supper being ended, 'or rather being come,' Jesus knowing that the Father had given all things into his hands, and that he was come from God, and went to God; he riseth from supper, and laid aside his garments; and took a towel, and girded himself, 'clothing himself with humility.' After that he poureth water into a basin, and began to wash the disciples' feet, and to wipe them with the towel wherewith he was girded. So after he had washed their feet, and had taken his garments, and was set down again, he said unto them, Know ye what I have done to you? The kings of the Gentiles exercise lordship over them; and they that exercise authority upon them are called benefactors. But ye shall not be so. But he that is greatest among you, let him be as the younger; and he that is chief, as he that doth serve. For whether is greater, he that sitteth at meat, or he that serveth? is not he that sitteth at meat? but I am among you as he that serveth. Ye call me Master and Lord: and ye say well; for so I am. If I, then, your Lord and Master, have washed your feet, ye also ought to wash one another's feet. For I have given you an example, that ye should do as I have done unto you. Verily, verily, I say unto you, The servant is not greater than his Lord; neither he that is sent greater than he who sent him. If ye know these things, happy are ye if ye do them."[81]

This kind of mutual subjection, readiness to serve one another, should characterize all the members of the church in their conduct to one another; but it should be especially prominent in the character and conduct of the office-bearers of the church. They ought never to forget, that though they are over their brethren in the Lord in one sense, in another they are not their lords; Christ Jesus is the Lord; they are their "servants for Jesus' sake."[82] Our Lord, aware of the tendency of superiority of rank to produce arrogance, warns his official servants against this hazard. "Be not ye called Rabbi; for one is your Master, even Christ; and all ye are brethren. Neither be ye called masters: for one is your Master, even Christ. But he that is greatest among you shall be your servant."[83] The same truth is suggested by the peculiar form of expression in the passage before us. "Ye juniors, submit yourselves to the elders" in the discharge of their official functions; "but"[84] this is not the only kind of submission that is required in the church—among Christians; "let all of you," whether elder or younger, seniors or juniors, official rulers or private members, "let all of you be subject one to another." Mutually do service; and let him who is most esteemed in the church be the readiest to serve.

CHAPTER TWO

OF THE MEANS OF PERFORMING THIS DUTY,— "THE BEING CLOTHED WITH HUMILITY"

Let us now, in the second place, consider the means by which Christians are to be enabled thus to be subject to one another. It is by being "clothed with humility." "Let all of you, being subject one to another, be clothed with humility." The idea plainly is, cherish and manifest humility; that will dispose and enable you to be subject one to another. But there is something peculiarly beautiful and instructive in the manner in which the idea is brought out. The Apostle, in the Epistle to the Colossians, calls on Christians to "put on," among other Christian virtues, "humbleness of mind," the same word rendered here "humility," as necessary to their "forbearing one another, and forgiving one another," which are just particular forms of being subject to one another. [85] The figure there is just the general one common in all languages.

The cultivation and display of a disposition is represented as the putting on and wearing a garment. But there is more in the phrase before us. The word rendered "Be clothed," is a remarkable one, occurring nowhere else in Scripture. It is borrowed from a piece of dress worn by servants when they were doing menial offices, a kind of apron fastened by strings, a piece of dress which at once intimated their station, and fitted them for the performance of its duties.[86] The Apostle calls on Christians, viewed as servants to each other, to put on humility as this piece of dress, to tie it on; just as he calls on them, as soldiers of the Captain of Salvation, to put on faith as a breastplate, and hope as an helmet. Cultivate humility, which will mark you as mutual servants, and fit you for mutual service. And it is difficult not to entertain the thought, that our Lord on the occasion already adverted to, putting on the towel like the servant's apron, and tying it around him, the visible emblem of his humility, and his readiness under its influence to serve, was before the Apostle's mind) and that he then remembered the words of the Lord Jesus, words he was not likely to forget, "I have given you an example that ye should do, as I have done to you." All that is necessary here in the way of illustration, is shortly to show what that humility is which the Apostle enjoins, and then in a few words to point out how it fits Christians for being "subject one to another."[87]

I. HUMILITY EXPLAINED

Humility, or, as the same word is elsewhere rendered more literally, "humbleness of mind," "lowliness of mind," is expressive of a low because a just estimate of ourselves—of our nature, of our character, of our condition, of our deserts.

The humble man has just, and therefore lowly, views of his own nature, as a *creature* infinitely inferior to, entirely dependent on, God; greatly inferior to angels, belonging to the lowest order of God's intelligent offspring; and, as a *sinner*, the proper object not only of the judicial displeasure of God, but of the moral disapprobation of all good and wise intelligences; inexcusably guilty, thoroughly depraved, righteously doomed to everlasting destruction; who, if saved at all, must owe his salvation to the riches of free grace, sovereign mercy.

The humble man has also just, and therefore lowly, views of his own individual character. He is sensibly impressed with the heinousness and aggravation of his own sins; he feels his own heart to be deceitful above all things, and desperately wicked; he knows that in him, that is, in his flesh, dwells no good thing. If his inward and outward man, his character and conduct, have been brought into any measure of conformity to the mind and will of God, he is aware that, so far as he is a new creature, he is "God's workmanship, created of him unto good works;" that "by the grace of God he is what he is;" that the work of renovation is very imperfect in him; and there is still very much wanting, very much wrong; and that, while he has much for which to be thankful, he has much of which to be ashamed, nothing of which to be proud.

And not only does the humble man form a low estimate of his nature generally, and of himself individually, when he tests human nature, and his own character and conduct, by the law of God, but he cherishes a humble opinion of himself, intellectually, morally, spiritually, in comparison with others. His tendency is to notice the excellences, rather than the faults, of others; while he looks at his own faults rather than at his excellences, and "in lowliness of mind he esteems others better than himself." He knows his own deficiencies and faults much more extensively and thoroughly than he can know those of other men; and the charity which always accompanies true humility, leads him to attribute what seems to be good in other men to the best principle which can reasonably be supposed to have produced it; while it leads him, from the necessary ignorance of their motives, to make allowances for their defects and failings, which he cannot make for his own. Humility does not lead a man to overlook or disclaim what God has done in him or by him, but leads him to give all the glory to Him to whom it is due; and while he cannot but see that God has made him to differ from others, and be deeply grateful for this, he at once feels that it is God alone who has done this; and is so sensible of the manner in which he has counterworked the Divine operations for his sanctification, that he is very ready to believe and acknowledge, that any other person blessed with his helps and advantages, would have greatly surpassed him in his attainments. When he thinks of what he is in comparison of what he ought to have been, in comparison of what he might have been, when he thinks of what others with far inferior advantages have attained to, and recollects that whatever is spiritually good in him has been put into his heart by the invincible, but not unresisted, efficacious operation of the Holy Ghost, he not only feels that he ought to lie very low before God, but that, even in reference to his fellow-men, he has nothing to boast of.

Humility has been well described as consisting in "the not being deluded with a false conceit of what we have not, not puffed up with a vain conceit of what we really have, nor affecting to be esteemed by others, either in their imagining us to be what we are not, or discerning us to be what we are."[88] Humility will not make us unconscious of what is good in us, but it will make us beware of imagining that to be good which is not, or that which is good to be better than it is; and it will constantly keep before the mind, that whatever good is in us, has been put into us, is not so much ours as God's, the gift of his grace, the work of his Spirit, and thus make the very consciousness of our sanctification, instead of puffing us up, a means of deepening the conviction, that no flesh may "glory in his presence," but that "he who glorieth must glory in the Lord."[89] Such is the humility with which the Apostle exhorts all Christians to be clothed, that they may be all subject one to another.

II. THE TENDENCY OF HUMILITY TO SECURE MUTUAL SUBJECTION

I have already adverted to the peculiar force of the expression," Be clothed." The command does not refer so much, if at all, to the manifestation of this disposition in demeanor and language, but rather to the cherishing of it in the heart, to the maintaining ofit in all circumstances, as that which fits a Christian for being subject to his fellow Christians, by serving them in love, like the servant who fastened his serving robes about him as necessary for the proper discharge of his duty as a servant. Humility is to the Christian, as the servant of all his brethren, what the appropriate dress for service was to the servant in common life. A proud, self-conceited man, is not disposed, is not qualified for serving others. He is continually making demands on others for service. It is their duty, in his estimation, to serve him, not his to serve them. A haughty mind ill comports with becoming all things to all men, pleasing our neighbor to his edification, in love serving each other, bearing one another's burdens, and so, in one word, fulfilling the law of Christ: just as a gaudy dress, a rich flowing robe, does not suit, is at once incongruous and inconvenient in one that serves. On the other hand the humble-minded man is ready to serve, feels honored in being permitted to do any office which can promote the honor of his Lord in the welfare of his brethren. Like the plainly, suitably-attired servant, he is like his work, and fit for it. He is ready to loose the latches of his Lord's sandals, and to wash his brethren's feet. The importance of humility, in order to the discharge of those offices which are so closely connected with the peace and spiritual prosperity of a church, is very strikingly manifested in the following exhortations of the Apostle Paul: "Be like-minded, having the same love, being of one accord, of one mind. Let nothing be done through strife or vain-glory; but in lowliness of mind let each esteem other better than themselves. Look not every man on his own things, but every man also on the things of others. Let this mind be in you, that was in Christ Jesus," the disposition to humble himself that he might serve others. "Put on, therefore, as the elect of God, holy and beloved, bowels of mercy, kindness, humbleness of mind, meekness, long-suffering; forbearing one another, and forgiving one another, if any man have a quarrel against any."[90]

CHAPTER THREE

OF THE MOTIVE URGING CHRISTIANS TO CULTIVATE HUMILITY

The only other topic in the text which requires consideration, is the motive employed by the Apostle to urge Christians to cultivate that humility which was so necessary to their mutually serving each other. "Be clothed with humility: for God resisteth the proud, and," or rather but [91], "giveth grace to the humble." The leading idea is, 'humility is the object of the approbation of God, and pride of his disapprobation; and he makes this very manifest in his dispensations respectively to the proud and to the humble.' As to any disposition or action, the first question with every man ought to be, the first question with a Christian will be, What is the estimate God forms of them; what effect will the cultivation of the one and the performance of the other have on my relations towards him? and the resolution of that question ought to have more influence with every man, with every Christian will have more influence, than all other things taken together, as to his checking or cherishing the disposition, following or avoiding the course of conduct. This matter is very clear as to pride and humility, "God resisteth the proud, but giveth grace to the humble." This is a quotation from the book of Proverbs, iii. 34, according to the Greek version in common use at the time; in our version, which is a literal rendering of the Hebrew original, it runs thus, "Surely he scorneth the scorners, but giveth grace to the lowly."

"God resists the proud." He sets himself to oppose them. It is impossible, in the nature of things, that God should not disapprove of pride, for it is a disposition which, just in the degree in which it prevails, unfits a man for his duty to God and to man, makes him a rebel to the one and an oppressor to the other; and, in any view we can take of it, it counteracts God's design to glorify himself in making his creatures happy. The Divine disapprobation against pride is strongly marked in an endless variety of ways. It is deeply impressed on the constitution of man as God's work, whether you consider the misery it inflicts on its subjects, or the disapprobation and dislike it produces in all who witness it. An apocryphal writer has said, "Pride was not made for man."[92] It may be, with equal truth said, Man was not made for pride. It is a disposition he cannot indulge without making himself unhappy. They sadly err who "count the proud happy." There is harmony in all God's works, and, to make man happy, his disposition must correspond to his condition; a proud being, who is at the same time a dependent being, entirely dependent on God, to a great extent dependent on his fellow-men, must be miserable. His whole life is a struggle to be and to appear to be what he is not, what he never can be.

The disapprobation of pride by God is evident, not only in his having so constituted man as that the proud man cannot be happy, but in his so constituting man as that the proud man is the natural object of disapprobation and dislike to all other men. No class of men are more disliked than proud men. And how could God more distinctly mark his disapprobation of pride, than by constituting human nature so, that the display of pride should excite in, and draw forth from men, sentiments directly opposite to those which the proud man wishes? He seeks admiration, he meets with contempt. No one really wishes to gratify the proud, and his mortification affords general satisfaction.

In the ordinary course of his providential dispensations, God so often shows his opposition to pride, that it has become a proverb, that 'a haughty spirit goeth before a fall;' and He has sometimes departed out of his usual mode of procedure, and miraculously shown how much he disapproves of haughtiness in man. Nebuchadnezzar, the proud king of Babylon, walked in the palace of his kingdom; and as he walked, he spake and said, "Is not this great Babylon, which I have built for the house of the kingdom, by the might of my power, and for the honor of my majesty?" How strikingly and effectually did God resist this proud man, and show that He, the King of heaven, all whose works are truth, and his ways judgments, is able to abase those who walk in pride! While the word was in the king's mouth, there fell a voice from heaven, "O king Nebuchadnezzar, to thee it is spoken, The kingdom is departed from thee: And they shall drive thee from men, and thy dwelling shall be with the beasts of the field: they shall make thee to eat grass as oxen, and seven times shall pass over thee, until thou know that the Most High ruleth in the kingdom of men, and giveth it to whomsoever he will. The same hour was the thing fulfilled upon Nebuchadnezzar; and he was driven from men and did eat grass as oxen, and his body was wet with the dew of heaven, till his hairs were grown like eagles' feathers, and his nails like birds' claws." Take another example: "Upon a set day Herod, arrayed in royal apparel, sat on his throne, and made an oration. And the people gave a shout, 'It is the voice of a god, and not of a man.' And immediately the angel of the Lord smote him, because he gave not God the glory: and he was eaten up of worms, and gave up the ghost."[93]

The plan of salvation through Christ is so framed as strikingly to show that "God resisteth the proud." No man can become a partaker of its blessings who does not "deny," renounce "himself." It is only as a being deserving, capable of deserving, nothing but punishment, and deeply sensible of this, that any man can obtain the pardon and peace, the holiness and comfort, of the Christian salvation. "The rich" in their own estimation "are sent empty away." Men, who are all naturally proud, must be "converted, and become" humble "like little children," else they cannot enter into the kingdom of heaven.[94] And just in that degree in which pride prevails, even in a regenerate man, will he fail to enjoy the consolation that is in Christ. The declarations of Scripture on this subject are very explicit, "Pride and arrogancy I hate. The Lord knoweth the proud afar off. The lofty looks of men shall be humbled, and the haughtiness of man shall be bowed down; and the Lord alone shall be exalted. For the day of the Lord of hosts shall be upon every one that is proud and lofty, and upon every one that is lifted up, and he shall be brought low."[95] "God," to borrow the words of Archbishop Leighton, "singles out pride as his great enemy, and sets himself in battle array against it, as the word is.[96] It breaks the ranks of men in which he hath set them, when they are not subject, as the word is before;[97] yea, it not only breaks rank, but rises up in rebellion against God, and doth what it can to dethrone him and usurp his place. Therefore, he orders his force against it; and so be sure, if God be able to make his party good, pride shall not escape ruin. He will break it, and bring it low; for he is set upon that purpose, and will not be diverted."

While God thus resists the proud, "he giveth grace"—that is, he shows favor—"to the humble." Humility is the object of his approbation, and he shows this by his conduct to those who are characterized by it. An humble state of mind, as in accordance with truth, and calculated to promote the true happiness both of the individual who cherishes it, and of all with whom he is connected, must be the object of the Divine approbation; and we have just to reverse the representation given of the manifestation of the state of the Divine mind, in reference to the proud, to see how he shows favor to the humble. He does so in the quiet and peace of mind which, from the very constitution of human nature, humility produces; and in the comparative freedom from ill-will, and enjoyment of the esteem and good wishes of others, which from the same constitution it secures. The more deeply a man realizes his insignificance as a creature, and his demerit as a sinner, his guilt and depravity and helplessness, the more readily does he embrace the gospel of God's grace, "the word of the truth of the gospel," and in it obtain possession of all heavenly and spiritual blessings. It is the man who knows and believes that he is a fool, that is made wise; the man who has no hope in himself, that obtains "good hope through grace;" the man who sees and feels that he is nothing but sin, that is "made the righteousness of God in Christ;" the man who loathes himself, that is "sanctified wholly in the whole man—soul, body and spirit." It is the man who most feels his own weakness, that is most "strengthened with all might in the inner man," and experimentally understands the spiritual paradox, "When I am weak, then am I strong." It is a remark, by one who was very intimately acquainted with the hidden life, "It is undoubtedly the secret pride and selfishness of our hearts that obstructs much of the bounty of God's hand, in the measure of our graces and the sweet embraces of his love, which we should otherwise find. The more that we let go of ourselves, still the more should we receive of himself. Oh, foolish we, that refuse so blessed an exchange!"[98] The passages of Scripture in which God declares his approbation of humility, and his delight in the humble, are very numerous. "Though the Lord be high, he has respect to the lowly. He forgets not the cry of the humble, he hears their desire; he prepares their hearts, he causes his ear to hear. Thus, saith the high and lofty One who inhabits eternity, whose name is Holy, I dwell in the high and holy place, with him also that is of a contrite and humble spirit, to revive the spirit of the humble, and to revive the heart of the contrite one." And this is the declaration of Him who came to reveal the character and will of his Father, and who was himself meek and lowly in spirit, "Whosoever shall exalt himself shall be abased; but he that shall humble himself shall be exalted. Blessed are the poor in spirit; for theirs is the kingdom of heaven."[99]

Leighton's paraphrase on "God giveth grace to the humble," is characteristically beautiful. "He pours it out plentifully on humble hearts. His sweet dews and showers slide off the mountains, and fall on the low valley of humble hearts, and make them pleasant and fertile. The swelling heart, puffed up with a fancy of fullness, has no room for grace, is not hollowed and fitted to receive and contain the graces that descend from above. And again, as the humble heart is most capable, as emptied and hollowed out it can hold most; so it is most thankful, acknowledges all as received. But the proud cries all is his own. The return of glory that is due for grace, comes most freely and plentifully from a humble heart. God delights to enrich it with grace, and it delights to return to him glory. The more he bestows on it, the more it desires to honor him withal; and the more it doth so, the more readily he still bestows more upon it. And this is the sweet interchange between God and the humble soul. This is the noble ambition of humility, in respect of which all the aspirings of pride are low and base. When all is reckoned, the lowliest mind is truly the highest; and these two agree so well, that the more lowly it is, it is thus the higher; and the higher thus, it is still the more lowly."

Surely this is a powerful motive for the cultivation of humility. What so much to be feared as God's disapprobation, and what so much to be desired as his favor? The command, "be ye clothed with humility," has great additional force from the consideration, that this was the chosen garb of our Lord and King, and chosen by him as that in which he could both best serve his Father and his people. Surely, to use the words of an old divine, "It is meet that we should remember, that the blessed Savior of the world hath done more to prescribe, and transmit, and secure this grace, than any other, his whole life being a great continued example of humility; a vast descent from the glorious bosom of his Father to the womb of a poor maiden; to the form of a servant, to the miseries of a sinner, to a life of labor, to a state of poverty, to a death of malefactors, to an untimely grave, to all the intolerable calamities which we deserved; and it were a good design, and yet but reasonable, that we should be as humble in the midst of our calamities and base sins, as he was in the midst of his fullness of the Spirit, great wisdom, perfect life, and most admirable virtues." [100]

And while the thought, that it is only by thus putting on humility that Christians can be mutually subject to and serve each other, and thus promote the peace and prosperity of the church on earth, should be felt as a powerful incentive to grow in this grace; we should remember, also, that the cultivation of this grace is a necessary preparation for the holy delights of the church above. They to whom, on that day when men's destinies shall be finally fixed, the universal Judge will say, "Come, ye blessed of my Father," are those who can scarcely recognize their own actions in those eulogized by him." And the exercises of heaven are such as only the humble can engage in with satisfaction. They fall down on their faces there before the throne and Him who sits on it; they cast their crowns at his feet. The only worthiness they celebrate is the worthiness of the Lamb that was slain; and the whole glory of their salvation is ascribed to Him, of whom, and through whom, and to whom, are all things. "Salvation to our God and to the Lamb forever and ever." We must be formed to the temper of heaven if we would be sharers in its joys. We must have the same mind in us as is in the holy angels and the spirits of the just made perfect, if we would be admitted to their society, and participate in their delights. Were we to carry pride with us to heaven, it would soon cast us out again, as it did the angels, who kept not their first estate. Let us then earnestly covet a large measure of this heavenly temper. Let it be our constant prayer, that the Spirit of all grace would so bring the truth before our minds, and keep it there, respecting our condition and character as creatures and sinners, sinners lost by their own inexcusable guilt, saved solely by the sovereign grace of God, as that every rising of undue self-complacency may be repressed, and that we may be enabled to "walk worthy of the vocation wherewith we are called, with all lowliness and meekness; with long-suffering, forbearing one another in love, endeavoring to keep the unity of the Spirit in the bond of peace." Oh, how happy the church, where all the elders and all the members are habitually under the influence of Christian humility! May that blessing, through the grace of Him who is exalted to be "Head over all things to his church," be increasingly ours! And to his name be all the glory.

Appendix A

How different was the spirit which animated those who pretended to be Peter's successors, appears strikingly in a remarkable story told in the Clementine Homilies:—

"Peter, wishing to establish in a bishopric, Zaccheus, who was backward to accept of it, cast himself at his feet, and entreated him to administer την αρχην—the princedom. 'I would readily do,' said Zaccheus, 'whatever a prince ought to do; but I am afraid to bear the name, because it exposes to so much envy as to be dangerous.' Peter consented that Zaccheus should not take the name of prince; but he gave him all the authority of one.

Και σου μεν εργον, said he, κελευειν; των δε αδελφων υπεικειν και μη απειθειν. 'It is your business to command; and, as to the brethren, it is theirs to submit to and obey you.'"

It is universally admitted that the Clementine Homilies are forgeries; but they are very authentic evidences of the spirit of the Roman Church at the time of their production. The bishops are there represented as Δυνασται, βασιλεις, δεσποται, κυριοι. How strangely does all this contrast with the words of the One Master,—"Call no man master on earth: be not ye called masters."—Hom. Clem, iii 63, 64, 66, p. 646.

APPENDIX B

"*Τῶν κληρῶν* plurale: singulare *ποιμνης. Ποιμνη μια.* Grex unus sub uno Pastore principe Christo: sed *κλῆροι* portiones multæ, pro numero locorum et antistitum.—Bengel.

This view throws light on the whole passage. Among the Nomadic tribes wealth consisted almost entirely in flocks and herds. The great proprietors were just shepherds on a great scale. Ἀρχιποιμένες, ποιμένες ὧν εἰσὶ τὰ πρόβατα ἰδια,[1] The whole *ποίμνη* (poimné: flock) belonged to them: but under them there were *ποιμένες*, each of whom had his own *κλῆρος* (kléros: a lot). The Ἀρχιποιμὴν (chief-shepherd) was often absent—but, on his coming to see his flocks, he would notice the manner in which the under-shepherds had treated *his* property, and deal with them accordingly.

"Vetustus quidem fuit ille loquendi modus, ut totum ordinem ministrorum clerum, vocarent: sed utinam Patribus nunquam venisset in mentem ita loqui: quia quod toti Ecclesiæ Scriptura communiter tribuit, minime consentaneum fuit ad pancos homines restringere." —Calvin.

"Clerus temporibus Apostolorum erant plebeii, quod apparet ex prima Petri Epistola majestuosa."—Scaliger.

"Cleros vocat non diaconos aut presbyteros, sed gregem qui cuique fortè contigit gubernandus ne quis existimet, Episcopis in Clericos interdictum dominium, in ceteros esse permissum. Et presbyteros hic Episcopos vocat. Nondum enim increverat turba sacerdotum; sed quot erant Presbyteri, totidem erant Episcopi."—Erasmus.

"Olim populus Israeliticus *κληρος*, sors, sive patrimonium Dei, Deut. iv. 20; ix. 29. Nunc populus Christianus; cujus singulæ partes ut fieri solet *εν ὁμογενεσι* idem nomen participant."—Grotius.

"*Κληρους* hereditates vocat Ecclesias singulas, quibus singuli pastores præficiuntur."—Suicer.

"All believers are God's clergy."—Leighton.

It deserves notice, that it is a verb derived from *κληρους* which is used, Acts xvii 4, to describe the association of the believers with Paul and Silas at Thessalonica— *προσεκληρωθησαν*. Our translators have preserved the reference in their version "consorted."

"*Κληρους* multi Latinorum interpretantur clericos; veruntamen longe probabilius est, per cleros intelligi gregis dominici portiones, quæ singulis Episcopis pascendæ ac regende velut sortito obtigerunt, juxta id quod Cyprianus dicit, Ecclesiam esse unam, cujus singulas portiones singuli Episcopi in solidum tenent."—Estius.

Vater takes a singular view of the meaning of the term here: "*Κληρων* plurali numero, non nisi, Acts i. 26, eodemque forsan signincatu et hic." In this case *κατακυρευειν των κληρων* would signify arbitrarily to overrule the votes, to disregard the will of the church, when manifested by their giving forth their *κληρους*.

Appendix C

A word of similar meaning (*Νεανισκοι*) is apparently used in the New Testament to signify common soldiers, Mark xiv. 51, as well as in the profane Greek (Polyb. iv. 16; iii. 62). A similar usage prevails in the Latin language, as to the word of corresponding meaning (*Juvenis*). We find the same thing in the Hebrew language: Abraham's armed servants are called "the young men" (נצרים), Gen. xiv. 24. We have the same use of the word, Jos. ii. 1; 2 Sam. ii. 14: "The word 'young', possesses, in the Christian usage of various languages, the sense of 'lay'—see Bolten."— Steiger.

"*Νεωτεροι* hic non videntur esse natu minores; nam opponuntur doctoribus, sed potius auditores et discipuli, eodem fere sensu, quo, Luc. xxii 26, *ὁ μειζων* et *ὁ νεωτερος* sibi opponuntur." Rosenmuller.

"*Νεωτεροι* opponuntur *πρεσβυτεροις* et ex lege oppositionis intelligendi sunt omnes reliqui qui exceptis Presbyteris ecclesiam constituerent."—Kuttner.

Schotanus, though obviously very averse, "a communi Doctorum sententia discedere videri," states very distinctly, and defends very successfully, what appears to me the true meaning:—"Hic per *juniores* intelligimus totam ecclesiam. Id autem probamus (1.) ex repetitione verbi *presbyteri*; (2.)

ex collatione in verbis: *similiter*; (3.) quia summissionem regimini opponit; (4.) quia passim Apostoli quando agunt de officiis in quibus mutuus est respectus, solent utrumque urgere. Si autem quis dicat nomen illud *juniores* repugnari, respondemus—nequam. Nonne Apostolus Paulus totam Ecclesiam Galaticam 'filiolos' vocat, Gal. iv. 19, et hæc ratio est, quia tum temporis præcipue Ecclesiæ præficiebantur qui provectioris ætatis erant."

"Per juniores autem hoc loco maxime intelligitur Grex qui pendet à pastoribus, quia pastores et presbyteri, maxima ex parte, electi fuerunt ex senioribus ætate, et proinde maxima pars gregis constabat ex junioribus."—Amesius.

APPENDIX D

"*Κομβος* nodus vinculum quo illigabantur manicæ præsertim in vestitu servorum."—Bengel. Grotius gives the following quotation from Pollux, lib. iv., which is quite to the point:— *Τη των δουλων εξωμιδι και ιματιδιον τι προσκειται λευκον, ὁ εγκομβωμα λεγεται.* Putting on the *εγκομβωμα*, was preparing in a becoming manner to act as a servant; assuming the appearance and preparing for the duties of the servile state. "*Εγκομβωμα* vestis humilis et servorum erat: qui cum breves tunicas quas *επωμιδας* vocant gestarent, super has *εγκομβωμα* induere solebant; palliolum vilissimum sed

candidum; quod et *επιβλημα* ut observant antiqui dicebant."—
Heinsius. Sac. Exercit. p.577.

ENDNOTES

1. *Πρεσβυτερος*

2. *νεώτερος*

3. Senor, seigneur.

4. Vitringa, Whately, Neander.

5. Eph iv. 11,12.

6. 2 Cor. ii. 16.

7. 1 Cor. xii. 28.

8. *Πρεσβύτερος*, id est, senior, eat nomen quod tribuitur Ministris Ecclesiæ, sive quia olim Ministri Ecclesiæ plerumque deligebantur, qui jam essent grandioris ætatis: sive potius quia Ministri Ecclesiæ moribus senes referre debent, iisque is tribuendus honor, qui senibus tribui solet; ita igitur nomen non est ætatis sed officii et dignitatis.—Suicer.

9. Acts xx. 17, 28 ; Tit. i 5-7.

Επειδη λανθανει τους πολλους ἠ συνηθεια, μαλιστα της καινης δικθηκης, τους επισκοπους πρεσβυτερος ονομαζουσα, και τους πρεσβυτερος επισκοπους, σημειωτεον τουτο εντευθεν (Acts xx. 17, 28) και εκ της προς Τιτον επιστολης και εκ της προς Τιμοθεον πρωτης. — Πρεσβυτερος και τους επισκοπους, και των πραξεων βιβλος οιδε λεγομενους.—In hunc loc.— Œcumenius.

10. *Ποιμανατε—επισκοπουντες.*

11. Phil. i. 1.

12. 1 John x. 11-14. Heb. iii. 6. 1 Pet. ii. 25.

13. Luke xii. 42.

14. John xxi. 15-17.

15. 2 Cor. iv. 2.; Col. i. 28.; 1 Cor. i. 23.; 2 Cor. iv. 5.;
1 Thess. ii. 4.; 1 Tim. iv. 13, 15; 1 Tim. vi. 20.; Tit. ii. 1, 8.

16. Rom. xv. 30. Eph. vi. 19. Col. iv. 3. 2 Thess. iii. 1.

17. Leighton.

18. Eph. i. 17-19; iii. 16-19.

19. Heb. xiii. 1,11, 24.; 1 Tim. iii. 5; v. 17.; Heb. xiii. 17.

20. Jer. xv. 15.; 1 Cor. iii 12-15.

21. Ezek. xxxiv. 4.; 2 Thess. v. 14.

22. "Dum pastores ad officium hortari vult, tria potissimum vitia notat, quae plurimum obesse solent: pigritiam, scilicet, lucri captandi cupidatem et licentiam dominandi. Primo vitio opponit alacritatem aut voluntarium studium: secundo liberalem affectum: tertio moderationem et modestiam qua eeipsos in ordinem cogant"— Calvin.

23. *Επισκοπουντες.*

24. 1 Phil. 14.;   2 Cor. ix. 7.

25. 1 Tim. i 12.; Isa. l. 5.; Psal. xl 7.; Luke xii. 50

26. 1 Cor. ix. 7-11.

27. Numb. xxii. 18.; 1 Sam. xii. 3.; Acts xx. 33.

28. Matt. xx. 25-28.; Luke xxii. 25, 26.; See Appendix A.

29. "Ea debet esse Pastoris vita ut non solum quicquid loquitur,

sed etiam quicquid agit, sit auditorum doctrina." —Gerhard.

"Monstrosa res est gradus summus et animus infimus; sedes prima et vita ima; lingua magniloqua et vita otiosa; sermo multus et fructus nullus; vultus gravis et actus levis; ingens auctoritas et nutans stabilitas." —Bernhard.

30. Acts xx. 34, 35.; 2 Thess. iii. 7.

31. John xiii. 13-17.

32. "Tres sunt ministeri ecclesiastici pestes *αεϛγια, αισχϛοϰεϛδεια* et *φιλοπϛωτεια.*" —Gerhard.

33. 2 Cor. v. 20.; Matt. xvi. 19.; Matt. xviii. 18.;

Matt x. 40.; John xiii. 20. Matt. xix. 28.;

Eph. ii. 20.; Rev. xxi. 14.

34. "Est autem eximia modestia, quod se *συμπρεσβυτερον*, ipse nominat, quem caput et principem apostolorum postea confinxerunt, et vicedeum adeo."—Semler.

35. Acts xiv. 22.

36. 1 Cor. i. 23.; Gal. vi. 14.

37. *Αυτοπται.*

38. Leighton.

39. 2 Pet. i. 16-18.; John xvii. 22.

40. Col. iii. 4.; 2 Thess. i. 10.

41. 2 Cor. iv. 14.; John xvii. 24.; Rom. viii. 17.

42. Rom. vi. 5,; Eph. ii. 6.

43. Ezek. xxxiv. 31.

44. Isa. xl. 11.; Ezek. xxxiv. 11-14.; John x. 28.

45. Deut. xxxii 9.

46. Eph. i. 18. 1 Pet ii 9.

47. See Appendix B.

48. Matt. xxvii. 20; xviii. 20.

49. Acts i 10, 11.

50. Tit. ii. 13.

51. Phil. iv. i.; 1 Thess. ii. 19.

52. Milton.

53. 2 Tim. iv. 1.; Acts xx. 28.; 1 Tim. i. 19; iii. 9; iv. 12.; Tit ii 15.; 1 Tim. vi. 11,12.; 2 Tim. i. 13.; Rev. iii. 11.; 1 Tim. vi. 13-16.

54 Ὁμοίως manifeste ostendit eosdem hic significari presbyteros: sicut antea Petrus de presbyterorum erga suas oves, sic nunc de ovium erga suoa πξοεσ τωτας officio disserit: quamobrem etiam recte Syrus interpres addidit affixum vestris.—Beza.

55. 1 Pet iii. 1, 7.

56. Eph. v. 22, 25; vi. 1, 4, 5, 9.; Col. iii. 18-22; iv. 1.

57. *Πξεσβυτεςοι (Πρεσβυτερος)*

58. Lev. xix. 32.

59. 3 John 4.

60. Luke xxii. 26.

61. See Appendix C.

62. Salmeron.

63. 1 Thess. v. 12, 13.; Heb. xiii. 17.

64. Eph. iv. 11.

65. Acts xx. 28.

66. Acts vi. 3, 4.

67. Owen on the Hebrews.—Vol. iv. p. 260. Fol. ed.

68. Rom. xii. 7.

69. Acts x. 33.

70. Heb. xii 15.

71. Pastor is Mr. F.'s word; but, we have seen, pastor and elder are synonymous.

72. Prov. xv. 10.

73. Heb. xiii. 17.

74. 1 Num. xi. 15.

75. Isa. lviii. 10, 11.

76. Rom. xii 10.; Phil. ii. 3.

77. Psal. cxli. 5.; Col. iv. 17.

78. Rom. xv. 2.; Eph. iv. 2.; Col. iii. 13.; 1Cor. x. 24.

79. 1Cor. ix. 20, 21.

80. Matt. xx. 28.

81. John xiii. 2-17.; Luke xxii. 24-27.

82. 2 Cor. iv. 5.

83. Matt. xxiii 8.

84. Δξ.

85. Col. iii. 12.

86. See Appendix D.

87. Col. iii. 12.; Phil. ii. 3.

88. Leighton.

89. 1 Cor. i. 29-31.

90. Phil. ii. 2-5.; Col. iii. 12, 13.

91. Δξ.

92. Ecclus. x. 18.

93. Dan. iv. 29-33.; Acts xii. 21-23.

94. Luke i. 53.

95. Prov. viii 13.; Psal. cxxxviii. 6.; Isa. ii. 11, 12.

96. Αντιτασσεναι.

97. Υποτασσόμενοι.

9.8 Leighton.

99. Psal. cxxxviii. 6; x. 12, 17.; Isa. lvii. 15; lxvi. 2.; Matt. xxiii. 12; v. 3.

100. Jeremy Taylor.

VISIT US FOR THESE FREE eBOOKS

Available at www.greatchristianbooks.com

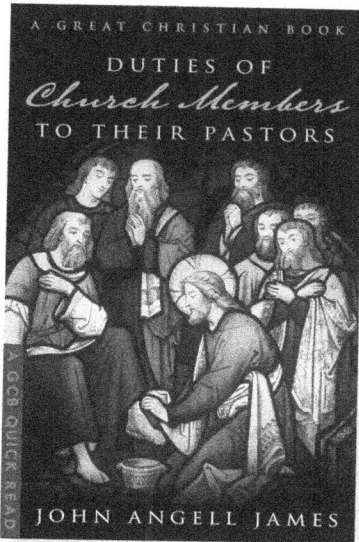

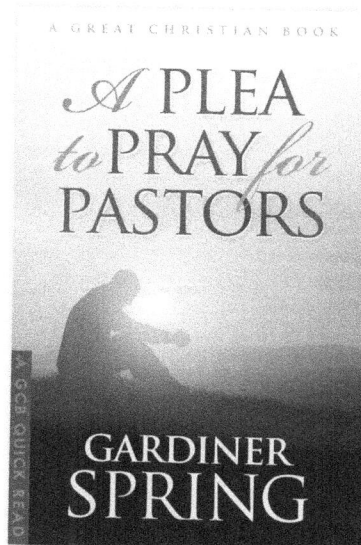

THE MISSION OF GREAT CHRISTIAN BOOKS

The ministry of Great Christian Books was established to glorify The Lord Jesus Christ and to be used by Him to expand and edify the kingdom of God while we occupy and anticipate Christ's glorious return. Great Christian Books will seek to accomplish this mission by publishing Gospel literature which is biblically faithful, relevant, and practically applicable to many of the serious spiritual needs of mankind upon the beginning of this new millennium. To do so we will always seek to boldly incorporate the truths of Scripture, especially those which were largely articulated as a body of theology during the Protestant Reformation of the sixteenth century and ensuing years. We gladly join our voice in the proclamations of— Scripture Alone, Faith Alone, Grace Alone, Christ Alone, and God's Glory Alone!

Our ministry seeks the blessing of our God as we seek His face to both confirm and support our labors for Him. Our prayers for this work can be summarized by two verses from the Book of Psalms:

"...let the beauty of the LORD our God be upon us, And establish the work of our hands for us; Yes, establish the work of our hands." —Psalm 90:17

"Not unto us, O LORD, not unto us, but to your name give glory." —Psalm 115:1

Great Christian Books appreciates the financial support of anyone who shares our burden and vision for publishing literature which combines sound Bible doctrine and practical exhortation in an age when too few so-called "Christian" publications do the same. We thank you in advance for any assistance you can give us in our labors to fulfill this important mission. May God bless you.

For a catalog of other great
Christian books including
other titles on ecclesiology—

contact us in
any of the following ways:

write us at:
Great Christian Books
160 37th Street
Lindenhurst, NY 11757

call us at:
(631) 956-0998

find us online:
www.greatchristianbooks.com

email us at:
mail@greatchristianbooks.com